STRONG
AT THE BROKEN
PLACES

STRONG
AT THE BROKEN
PLACES

UNITED STATES SENATOR
MAX CLELAND

LONGSTREET PRESS
Atlanta, Georgia

Also by Max Cleland:

Going for the Max!: 12 Principles for Living Life to the Fullest

STRONG

AT THE BROKEN

PLACES

*"The world breaks everyone and afterward many
are strong at the broken places."*

— ERNEST HEMINGWAY

Published by
LONGSTREET PRESS
2140 Newmarket Parkway
Suite 122
Marietta, GA 30067

Printed in the United States of America

1st printing 2000

Library of Congress Catalog Card Number: 00-105161

ISBN: 1-56352-633-6

Jacket and book design by Burtch Bennett Hunter
Front cover photograph by Joe Sports

To My Parents

"I can remember stepping out of the pediatric clinic into a corridor filled with 40 to 50 litter cases [from Vietnam], walking past them and joking when I could, but not feeling particularly involved. At first, when it was all new, I was glad they were your children, not mine. After a while, I changed. These kids were so brave, they endured so much, were so uncomplaining, you couldn't help but feel proud of them. . . .

They were worried, every one of them, not about the big things, not about survival, but how they would explain away their lost legs or the weakness in their right arm. Would they embarrass their families? Would they be able to make it at parties with guys who were still whole? Could they go to the beach, and would their scars darken in the sun and offend the girls? Would they be able to get special cars? Above all, and underlying all their cares, would anybody love them when they got back?"

Dr. Ronald J. Glasser
Major, U.S. Army Medical Corps
From his book *365 Days*

CONTENTS

FOREWORD

The hard uses of life oblige most of us to seek inspiration from stories of courage and faith that instruct us not only how to endure but how to prevail over misfortune. What follows is such a story, written well and poignantly by a man whom I am proud to call my friend.

Max Cleland caught a tough break in war. He has suffered greatly for his country, and his country should be grateful to him. But *Strong at the Broken Places* is not a demand for compensation or pity. Quite the opposite, it is a testimony of hope for those who despair, of courage for those who fear, of love for those who resent.

Raised by a loving family in the best country in the world, young Max Cleland could once look contentedly toward a future of unlimited possibilities. Before Vietnam, he lived a good life. Amazingly, after Vietnam, he has lived an even better one.

Early in his life, Max gave more than most to his country. What a credit to America that in rebuilding his own life, he chose to devote it to his country. He has served as Georgia's Secretary of State, as Director of the Veterans Administration, and as a United States Senator with distinction, demonstrating every day the courage and patriotism for which he is so widely admired. It is a pleasure and an honor to serve with him. When the vagaries of public life, and the partisanship and occasional pettiness that afflict our national affairs discourage me, I look to Max to help me remember why I came to Washington.

Max tells his story unsparingly, sharing with the reader the fear he felt in war and all the pain he suffered when the full horror of war became his personal misfortune. But even in the worst moments, his humor, optimism, and decency come vividly through. It is those qualities you will remember from this book and be inspired by as I have.

I have been privileged to spend much of my life in the company of heroes. I have never known a greater one than Max Cleland. He is a hell of a man whose extraordinary story humbles me as it will humble you. When vanity gets the better of me, I know to thank God for always helping me to recognize a better man when I see one. When you have finished this book, you will have met one, too.

United States Senator John McCain

A NEW BEGINNING: THE REST OF THE STORY

KHE SANH, VIETNAM
APRIL 8, 1968.

"I jumped to the ground, ran in a crouch until I got clear of the spinning helicopter blades, turned around and watched the chopper lift.

"Then I saw the grenade. It was where the chopper had lifted off.

"*It must be mine*, I thought. Grenades had fallen off my web gear before. Shifting the M-16 to my left hand and holding it behind me, I bent down to pick up the grenade.

"A blinding explosion threw me backwards."

I have been given a fresh start, a new beginning for the rest of my life. This book, when I wrote it twenty years ago, charted my story so far: my early years in public service and my struggle to find a purpose in life as an injured young Vietnam veteran. I have now had the benefit of another twenty years' worth of living and reflection, during which I have learned so many valuable lessons and have had truths revealed to me in amazing ways.

So, before you read *Strong at the Broken Places*, I need to tell you where I am now and some of the things that have happened to me in the years since this book was first published. Then, I want to share with you how God has given me a new beginning.

I have heard it said that the value of living a long time is that you get to see how things turn out. More than thirty-two years after that fateful day, April 8, 1968, and the grenade blast that changed my body and challenged my life for the rest of my days, I have to say that things have turned out pretty well for me.

Professionally, which in my case means politically, I have been able to live a life I could have only dreamed of growing up in my hometown of Lithonia, Georgia. My four years as head of the Veterans Administration under President Carter were exhausting but extremely satisfying. Given my own mixed experiences in VA hospitals, I rejoiced at the chance to improve the standards by which other veterans would be treated. One of the programs I instituted during my time in office was the VA Vet Center readjustment counseling program. I would discover, years later, that this program helped save the life of someone who had once helped me in a very important way. In addition, I helped improve VA medical care and expand the GI Bill, which I believe were pivotal improvements to the VA as a whole. As a veteran who struggled every day to overcome my own wounds, there was no greater reward than knowing I was helping people like myself all over the country to lead better lives.

After heading the VA, I returned to Georgia and made a successful bid in 1982 for the office of Georgia's Secretary of State. I was reelected twice, and I thought I would be in that office for the rest of my life. Most of my friends did, too. While in office, I cut red tape for small business people and implemented the national Motor Voter law, which added one million Georgians to the voter registration rolls. Holding such a public position forced me to continue striving to heal myself. My career was always challenging me, physically and mentally; I was never allowed to become discouraged by what I could not do. My schedule and responsibilities demanded that I lead as normal a life as possible if I was to do my job effectively. I served as Georgia's Secretary of State for a dozen fine years. As much as I enjoyed my job and the opportunities it gave me, by the early 1990s I was beginning to feel the need for a new challenge.

In the back of my mind, I knew I would love the chance to one day sit in the U.S. Senate and take Sam Nunn's seat on the Senate Armed Services Committee. Nunn had succeeded as senator the venerable Georgia statesman and national expert on defense matters, Richard Russell. Nunn eventually succeeded Russell as the Chairman of the Senate Armed Services Committee as well. In my mind, seeking to replace Sam Nunn in the Senate, taking his seat on the Armed Services Committee, and dealing with matters concerning our armed forces and America's commitments of those forces around the world were all aspirations that seemed tailor-made for me. Although Nunn seemed entrenched in the office, I knew that if the opportunity ever arose, I would try to succeed him.

Eventually, I got my chance. In October 1995, before a packed audience in the Georgia State Capitol Senate Chambers where I had gotten my start in the early 1970s, Nunn announced that he would not run for reelection. Within a week, I was in the race to succeed him. After four years as a Georgia State Senator in the early 1970s, four years as head of the Veterans Administration under President Carter in the late 1970s, and twelve years as Georgia's Secretary of State in the

1980s and early 1990s, I finally had the opportunity of a life-time. I ran for the U.S. Senate.

In a grueling and brutal campaign in which I was outspent 3.5 to 1, I eked out a victory in the 1996 race. My platform was based largely upon my plans to continue representing Georgia veterans and military personnel in the Russell/Nunn tradition and be a good public servant. Despite the challenges of the campaign, I let nothing discourage me from my ultimate goal. When the election results came in, I was ecstatic! Who would have believed if they'd seen me sitting in that amputee ward in Walter Reed Hospital all those years ago that I would one day become a United States Senator? It was a dream come true.

Additionally, after I was sworn in on January 7, 1997, I landed a seat on the Senate Armed Services Committee. Since then, I have been a part of the living history of my time. I have had a front-row seat on that history. I have relished every minute of it.

I arrived in the Senate in 1997 with some very definite goals. I wanted to continue to support a strong defense, reform our dependency on money in campaigns, and support progres-sive change to keep the economy moving.

Every day I serve is a proud day for me, both as an American and as a disabled veteran. The members of the Senate do not treat me any differently than they do any other colleague. That is a powerful incentive for me to keep myself involved and my voice heard. I am so grateful to be able to bring my per-spective to the table on issues that matter for so many people. To be a part of the American political process is a very humbling and wonderful thing. It is also an enormous personal challenge.

I live a schizophrenic life. I spend 50 percent of my time in Washington, D.C., and 50 percent of my time back in Georgia serving my constituents and campaigning. When I can, I travel abroad and visit our military forces scattered around the globe.

It's a pretty impossible schedule, but I love it. I cherish the opportunity to do what I now consider my life's work. I greatly admire the role our Founding Fathers cut out for the Senate in the U.S. Constitution. For me, the challenge of being a good senator is a lifetime challenge. It is much like infinity; you never seem to reach it, but you are always striving to touch it. I love that kind of life. I want to stay in the Senate for the rest of my public career.

Personally, my life has not always been as smooth. I have had to buckle down to fight middle-age sprawl. I encounter daily the "battle of the bulge" around my waist. I have had to lose a lot of weight, discipline myself to exercise and diet, and otherwise get in shape to meet the demanding schedule of being a U.S. senator. It has been rugged, but it has not been altogether bad for me. I am probably in the best shape mentally and physically that I have been in thirty years.

On a deeper emotional level, I still struggle with the aftermath of Vietnam every day. Like so many other veterans of that war, it will not be over for me until I am six feet under. The challenge of dealing with the loss of two limbs and my right hand (I was right-handed) is one I have adapted to, but will never get over. It is a battle I can fight and overcome, but one I will never completely win. From time to time, it gets me down. That is why I am always searching for inspirational quotes, stories, and role models to uplift my spirits, to keep me moving ahead and living my life to the fullest. I even published a book with my favorite anecdotes and quotes entitled *Going for the Max!: 12 Principles for Living Life to the Fullest*. It is just another tool I use to remind myself each day that I've been blessed to have life itself, and I should live it to the max!

Over the last thirty-two years, I have been able to heal a lot of the broken places in my life. The fact that I have been able to do so is attributable only to the grace of God and the love of friends. They have helped me survive. They have also helped me thrive. With their aid, I have been able to deal with the "slings and arrows of outrageous fortune" and the "thousand shocks that flesh is heir to," as Shakespeare put it, to move on and accomplish my goals.

But, up until 1999, there was one place in my psyche that had not healed. It was a place down deep that I felt would always be broken. It had to do with the grenade accident that cost me my limbs all those years ago. There were so many details about the explosion that I still did not know. I had never really known where the grenade had come from; I had never known for sure if it was mine or not. I had always assumed it probably had been my grenade. Therefore, every time I thought about the incident, I blamed myself for getting wounded, for not coming back from the war whole, for somehow "screwing up." For thirty-two years, I had carried around the weight of that uncertainty. When I was having a bad night, the lingering self-doubt could keep me awake for hours.

Then, one day in 1999, the History Channel interviewed me for a TV program they were doing on combat medics. I told the interviewer that I would never have made it to the Senate had it not been for the combat medics on the battlefield and the wonderful soldiers who helped save my life that day near Khe Sanh. I particularly had praise for those whom I'd thought had come to my side right after the explosion. I also made mention of the fact that I thought the grenade that exploded was one of mine that had dropped off my web gear while I was jumping out of the helicopter onto the landing zone.

The History Channel ran the broadcast in March 1999. A few days after the program aired, I got a phone call. I did not recognize the name of the caller on the other end of the line. My secretary, Amy Kimball, put him through anyway.

"Hi, this is Max Cleland. Can I help you?"

"Yes. My name is David Lloyd. I have something to tell you. I saw the History Channel broadcast. It wasn't your grenade. It was the grenade of the guy behind you."

I was taken aback for a brief moment. I didn't know what to say. I thought at first it was a crank call. "How do you know it was not my grenade?" I asked quizzically.

"I was there," he replied. "I was the first to you after the grenade went off."

I was stunned—as stunned as if another grenade had just gone off beside me. I had never met or even known the names of those who had come to my aid and put me on a medevac helicopter that day.

"You were the first one to me?" I challenged quickly, my mind racing. I knew I was going to need some sort of confirmation. This voice on the other end of the phone was going to have to prove it to me.

"Yes, I took off my web belt and made a tourniquet to stop the bleeding on one of your legs. I started cutting your uniform off to make strips to provide a tourniquet for the other leg."

That did it for me. Only someone who had been there that day would have known about cutting off the trousers of my uniform to make a tourniquet. One of my vivid memories right after the accident was of someone doing just that. I'd always thought it was such a strange thing to do. A soldier's uniform is considered sacred, a part of their personal space that other men don't mess with. I remembered feeling naked when my uniform was being cut off me at the time. But David had probably saved my life by doing so.

This guy must be real, I thought. *He is not kidding.* I couldn't speak. Time stood still as I sat there in my Senate office on that cold March day. My heart pounded with the anticipation of what I was about to hear. For the first time in more than three decades, I was going to learn the full story of what happened on that fateful day on a landing zone just east of Khe Sanh, the day the First Air Cavalry Division finally broke the longest siege of the Vietnam War. My questions would finally be answered.

My mystery caller David Lloyd, I learned, had been a marine mortar man in the war. Needless to say, he and I have since become fast friends. I have visited him numerous times at his home in Annapolis, Maryland. Besides enjoying David's company, early on I was on a mission to get the true story of what had happened to me that day. And David was only too happy to oblige.

In April 1968, David Lloyd was located with the Marines on a hill east of Khe Sanh. It was a hill held jointly by the Marines and the Army. The Army had set up a signal detachment on the hill. I had flown by helicopter into the landing zone with a radio relay team, attempting to set up a relay from the hill to my infantry battalion, which was moving into the Marine base at Khe Sanh miles away.

As I landed with my small team and radio equipment, I jumped off the chopper, hit the ground, and ran out from under the blades, looking back to see if everything and everybody was clear of the Huey. Unbeknownst to me, a young enlisted man who was only a day or two in country dropped a grenade while leaping off the helicopter. Unfortunately for me, he had straight- ened out the pins on all his grenades ahead of time, thinking they would be easier to pull out in case of enemy attack. However, as an inexperienced soldier, he didn't understand that this made him a walking bomb. Any jiggle or movement and a live grenade could fall loose from his pack.

David Lloyd said that after he tended to me and left me ashen white, bleeding, legs smoking from the explosion, he thought, "He's not going to make it." When the grenade went off, tearing my body apart, it also sprayed the young enlisted man with shrapnel. A Navy corpsman attached to the Marines,

Steve Johnson, came to my side and asked David to go tend to the other soldier. Meanwhile, another marine, Charlie Walton, started applying bandages to my right arm.

A few yards away, David approached the enlisted soldier filled with shrapnel. David said the young man was sobbing, "It's all my fault! It's all my fault! It was my grenade!" David put about twenty-five patches on the soldier to stop the bleeding from his shrapnel wounds. He noticed the young man still had on his body two grenades with the pins straightened out. David carefully removed them, since those two grenades could easily have killed us all.

Although he had remembered my name and had followed my career in public service over the years, David Lloyd never expected to see me again. When he watched the History Channel program in March 1999 and realized I didn't know it was someone else's grenade that had hurt me, he decided it was time to get in touch with me. Words cannot express how glad I am that he did.

David has given me an invaluable gift, the gift of peace of mind. By eliminating the mystery of that horrible accident, he has enabled me to get stronger at a particular broken place within myself that has nagged me for so long. I always believed that I had perhaps been to blame for the way the war turned out for me. Knowing the truth has given me a calm that I've never had before. Finally, I can say, "It was not my fault." That is a great burden off my shoulders. It makes all the other burdens in my life seem less significant and more manageable.

I know I was wounded in a freak accident of war, a circumstance of men acting the best way they knew how under the awful pressure, stress, fear, and fatigue of combat. I can accept my fate more easily now. My friend, the Senate chaplain Dr. Lloyd Ogilvie, has a saying that is one of my favorites: "Things don't work out. God works out things." I certainly believe He has done so in my life.

Since that phone call from David Lloyd, I have been in contact with both Steve Johnson and Charlie Walton, the two other men who helped save my life. It has been a rewarding experience for all of us, but probably especially so for me. Charlie told me that in the mid-1980s, he used the Vet Center readjustment counseling program I'd started at the VA to meet his own needs. He credits the program with saving his life. What a wonderful feeling it is for me to know that I have in some way repaid the favor to Charlie that he first bestowed upon me thirty-two years ago.

As I reflect upon this chapter in my life that has caused me so much pain, sorrow, and tears—and that still produces agony enough to take me to prayer each day—I praise the Lord for the good things He has given me that I still have left: life, the capacity to enjoy it, great friends to help make it worthwhile, and the continuing grace of God, who works out things and strengthens us even at the most broken places in our lives.

1

THE CHOICE

"Life is either a daring adventure or nothing."

— HELEN KELLER

The explosion stunned me. A loud ringing hammered in my ears, and I was afraid to look at my hand. Was it still there?

A voice called from the house: "Son, be careful with those firecrackers."

I looked at my hand; it appeared to be intact though it was numb. I had gone against my mother's warning not to light firecrackers in my hand. It was exciting to throw them—but this one had exploded in my fingers.

My hand began to throb. I snuffed the smoldering punk stick into the soft, Georgia earth and stuffed the pack of Zebra-brand firecrackers into my jeans pocket. Then I hurried into the house and ran cold water over my hand at the kitchen sink. As it began to feel better, so did my wounded pride. *A firecracker couldn't hurt me!*

As far back as I could remember I wanted to live life to the fullest. There was a deep, inner urge to challenge my limitations, to reach as high as I could, to be all I could be.

My earliest memory is as a four-year-old child learning to break out of my parents' dark, dreary, one-bedroom apartment in Atlanta. This was during World War II, and my father was overseas in the Navy. My mother worked as a secretary, and her mother stayed with me during the day.

My escape strategy was simple. Grandmother would encourage me to take an afternoon nap by lying down beside me, and she invariably fell asleep. As soon as I heard her soft snoring, I slipped out of bed and crept to the back of the apartment. The back door bolt was locked and out of my reach, but with a broomstick I learned how to push it back and open the door. Then I sped outside where I ran and jumped exuberantly in the sunshine.

When they installed a key-lock to foil me, I would slip the screen out of the ground-floor bedroom window and leap to the pavement. I would race up and down the sidewalk, exulting in my freedom. Grandmother would wake up terror-stricken, petrified that I might have run into the busy street. She would hail the nearest stranger and beg him to catch me. But I wasn't afraid at all; to me the sidewalk and the street represented freedom. I delighted in just being outside.

When my father returned from the war, he used the GI Bill to get a home loan on a small, two-bedroom, white-frame bungalow on Main Street in Lithonia, Georgia. Our home had big trees for swings and a large backyard where I could run and play. Twenty miles east of Atlanta, Lithonia had been Dad's hometown, and many of our relatives lived nearby. Some were descendants of the original Clelands who had emigrated from Scotland and Ireland in the 1700s.

A stocky, affable person with a lot of personality and warmth, my father began work as a salesman, a career he pursued throughout his life. My mother, a tall, dark-haired beauty with a pleasant smile and an affectionate disposition, continued to work as a secretary. Hugh and Juanita Cleland had one central objective: to provide a good life for their son, their only child.

Loving the outdoors I was inevitably drawn to sports. Dad erected a basketball backboard near the garage, and I would dribble, whirl, and toss a nearly worn-out basketball at the hoop until it was too dark for me to see.

One afternoon I looked up from shooting baskets to see a strange boy standing at our back fence. Tall and freckled, he was obviously a few years older than I.

"Hi," he called, "I'm Edgar Abbott. Can I shoot a few?"

His family lived a block away, and he, too, was an only child. We soon became inseparable. But Edgar had a two-year edge on me. Whereas many of my shots would bounce off the rim, Edgar always seemed to sink his with that satisfying "swish."

I hated getting beaten constantly by Edgar in basketball and the other games he introduced me to—baseball, tennis, and football. I was determined to bring my skills up to his level despite the age difference.

One day after school, he picked up the basketball and with his left hand hooked it effortlessly into the basket. Then he tossed the ball to me. "Now you do it."

"But I'm right-handed," I complained.

"So am I," said Edgar, "but I learned to shoot lefty. No telling when you'll need to use your left hand like this, especially when a big guy is guarding you."

Hour after hour I worked on my left-hand shot. I had to learn the proper twist of my wrist, and develop supple fingers with a light touch on the ball.

Soon I discovered something; footwork was important, too. Since a right-hand hook shot came off the left foot, I had to learn to shoot left-handed off my right foot and to spring high off my feet for the shot. Finally, the day came when I could sink a left hook-shot almost as easily as a right.

Edgar was a good teacher. He was also my personal coach.

I made the junior-high basketball team, and one night as we prepared to play another school, Edgar, now in high school, took me aside. "Max," he said, "I expect you to be high-point man tonight."

I stared at him blankly. But that night I ended up as the top scorer with 15 points—including several left-handed hook shots. I walked home in a daze. All those hours of practice, all that time trying to beat Edgar had paid off.

When I entered high school, my imagination was captured by the award given each year at graduation to the "outstanding senior." Nominations were based on proficiency in scholastics, athletics, and other school activities. The winner was given a large loving cup by the *Atlanta Journal* newspaper.

The cup appealed to me because it stood for many achievements. I didn't want to put all my efforts into either academics or athletics. I wanted to be good at everything.

And so I broadened my interests to include music and drama. I played the trumpet; I tried out and got parts in school plays; and on the side, I became involved in church activities.

In the 1950s, being raised in a Christian home and attending church was part of small-town culture. I eventually joined the Methodist Church in downtown Lithonia, but I visited other churches as well. I especially remember visiting one of the Southern Baptist churches just out of town on many occasions as a small boy. I vividly remember the short ride with my parents down a narrow blacktop road, the pungent scent of road tar mixing with the sweet aroma of honeysuckle. As we'd near the little, white-frame building, its ancient bell would be clanging, and I'd hear the organ playing the old revival hymns.

Inside, the pastor would greet me with the bone-crushing

grip he'd developed from his daily work as a carpenter. We'd find a place to sit on one of the long wooden pews, and my shirt would soon be sticking to the heat-softened varnish. I'd lean back and listen to the music and the pastor's sermon. Many Sundays his words stirred my deepest emotions.

This pastor occasionally issued a call for us to come forward and be "saved." Several times as a small boy, I joined those who went up to the altar after the sermon. Yet, I was never quite sure what this action on my part really meant.

During my high school years I tried to sort it all out. God was a vague entity in my life whereas the world of athletics, school plays, and dating pretty girls was very real. A decision to live my life for God seemed to mean I should give up the pleasures I enjoyed. Or did it? Didn't God want me to do my best and be the best?

We all make choices during our teen years, and I made mine. The religious life was fine for those who needed it. I believed in God, I belonged to the church—but the world was what I wanted to explore. I wanted to meet it head-on. I wanted to test it to the outer limits. I wanted to try everything.

Two things happened to solidify this decision. In the Lithonia City Tennis Championships, I finally, for the first time, beat Edgar Abbott at tennis.

And in June of 1960, at age 17, standing in the hot summer night at our outdoor high school graduation, I was presented the *Atlanta Journal*'s heavy silver loving cup as Lithonia High School's "Outstanding Senior."

I was on my way.

2

MASTER OF MY FATE

"Do not grieve for me as I depart
Me and my reckless, pioneering heart."

— ANONYMOUS

The desire to test my limits was only partially achieved in college. At Stetson, a small liberal arts college in central Florida, I battled for two years just to survive academically. In my junior year I switched my major for the third time—to history.

This proved to be a turning point in my life. For through the study of American history, I became deeply interested in politics. I applied and was accepted for a semester's study at American University in Washington, D.C. Hungry for a new adventure in my life, I found it in Washington.

On September 10, 1963, I eagerly watched Washington National Airport come into view from my plane's window. As we neared the city, I saw the Capitol in the distance and even spotted the White House where President John Kennedy was in office. The excitement grew inside me.

One bright autumn afternoon I got a glimpse of the president himself; he rode in an open convertible progressing slowly up Pennsylvania Avenue in a parade for the emperor of Ethiopia, Haile Selassie. The emperor, in regal uniform, stood beside the sitting president, but as I stretched on tiptoes in the crowd my attention was fastened on Kennedy's smiling, suntanned face.

Weeks later I was one of a small group of fellow students who were allowed to visit the president's office when he was out of town. My heart pounded as I stepped into the famous Oval Office with its pale blue walls.

Immediately, I spotted Kennedy's much-publicized rocking chair. In front of his huge desk were two love seats with a little rug between them. To the left was a bookcase which held photos of his wife and children, plus a model of a sailing ship. I walked over to the desk and stood there trying to comprehend the power inherent in the presidency. I couldn't.

Three days later President John Kennedy was dead.

In grief, I felt compelled to go to that spot on Pennsylvania Avenue where I had watched him pass by in the parade. As a cold, November wind blew brown leaves and wastepaper along the sidewalk, I felt an overwhelming sense of man's perishability. Yet at the same time I had a sudden, compelling inner drive to serve my country.

Back at Stetson for my senior year, I recall one night when I knew I had to ask myself certain questions. *Who am I, really?* I thought. *What kind of stuff am I made of?* The hour was late, and only the soft snoring of my roommate broke the silence.

I switched off my desk lamp and looked out into the faint Florida night which outlined palm trees against the horizon. My neck tingled. Something was waiting for me out there. I knew it. Then a phrase from one of Tennyson's poems came to my mind: "Drink life to the lees."

That was what I wanted, more than awards or power—more than anything. I wanted to "drink life to the lees"—to taste life to the fullest! As part of this zest for new adventure, I'd already signed up for the Army Reserve Officers Training Corps (ROTC). I had taken an extra course in the tactics of fighting a guerrilla war. The U.S. was getting more involved in a little country the Army major pointed out on the map one morning. "Veet-naamm" he called it. Soon I was reading more and more about this country in the news.

As a part of the ROTC program, I had gone to Fort Benning, Georgia, home of the U.S. Army Infantry School, for some basic training, tests, leadership challenges, and simulated combat maneuvers.

As I moved my gear into the barracks that first day, a tremendous roar shook the building. I dashed outside to watch giant, olive-drab helicopters almost blacken the sky.

A sergeant was crossing the dusty lot as the helicopters churned by. When the roar faded, he said, "That's the 11th Air Assault Test Division. It's a new Army experimental unit." He pointed across the company street to its headquarters. "They're testing helicopters to find out how they might be used in 'Veet-naamm.'"

As the choppers continued to roar in and out of the 11th Air Assault area all that day and much of the night, I watched them whenever I could. Soon this would become the First Air Cavalry Division, and the possibility of seeing action with them sent my adrenalin pumping. Some day I would join them, I promised myself.

After graduating from Stetson and taking a year of graduate study at Emory University in Atlanta, I eagerly joined the Army on active duty. I wanted to become a signal officer, and I was sent to learn the signal school basics. While there, I applied for a paratrooper training course.

A young fellow officer kidded me: "Don't you know, Max, that the standard rule for staying out of trouble in the Army is to never volunteer for anything?"

I just stared at him, almost in contempt.

My orders came through, and I was to report for jump school back at Fort Benning, Georgia. After three of the most physically punishing weeks of my life, I stood at the open side of a troop plane in a roaring blast of air staring at a hazy earth 1,200 feet below me. Before diving into that blue nothingness, I wondered for a split second if I was a fool to keep reaching out for new adventures. Was this really what life was all about?

Then I jumped. It was exhilarating. Even as my chute snapped open I knew I wanted to taste more!

Back in signal school in Fort Monmouth, New Jersey, I got my chance to volunteer for duty with the First Air Cavalry Division whose men were now fighting in the jungles of Vietnam. By now—1966—285,000 American men were battling for their lives in a war that had exploded like hot grease in a kitchen conflagration. Radio men were vital to the war, and there weren't enough of them to go around. My volunteering was inevitable.

I filled up several pages with reasons why I wanted to join the First Cav.

"Air mobility is the wave of the future," I stated, explaining that as a history student I was keenly aware of the French military mistakes in Indochina. "It is the way to fight a war of national liberation in the underdeveloped world," I continued, presenting my belief that American technology in helicopter operations would defeat North Vietnam. A new chapter was being written in American history, and I wanted to help write it.

I was firmly set on my course when there was a surprising interruption. A junior officer approached me one day and asked me if I knew the new commander of the signal center and school, Brigadier General Tom Rienzi.

I shook my head.

"Well, he would like to talk to you."

"What for?"

"To see if you'd be interested in being his aide."

That was a shocker. "But why me?"

"Your statement requesting service in Vietnam appealed to the colonel who is screening out prospects for the general."

"I'd rather go to Vietnam."

"Will you give it some thought?"

"It won't hurt to see him, I guess."

Two days later my orders to join the First Air Cavalry in Vietnam came through. I sat in the classroom holding them, torn between going to Vietnam, a known assignment that I wanted, and working with the general, an unknown assignment that I didn't know whether I wanted or not. I jammed the orders into my pocket. I would go to Vietnam; the general could get someone else to be his aide-de-camp.

The next day I was summoned to the general's office for the interview. It didn't look like an Army office except for some military pictures and insignia on the paneled walls. The secretaries, busy at electric typewriters, were all civilians. Their mahogany desks sank into two-inch-thick, beige carpeting. It could have been a plush executive suite anywhere in the country. Did I really want to spend my Army time in a place like this? Not me! That was certain.

The intercom buzzed. One of the secretaries answered, then looked up and smiled. "You may go in now, Lieutenant."

"Hi, I'm Tom Rienzi," boomed a deep voice as I stepped inside the office. I was a bit startled as the general bounded out from behind his desk and stuck out his hand, bending his shoulder just enough to flash the biggest star I'd ever seen. I had never been in the presence of a general officer before. I'd only seen them played in movies by John Wayne or Gregory Peck.

I didn't know whether to salute or not in view of the general's outstretched hand.

My hand shot up to my forehead. My heels clicked together. I stood frozen. "Lieutenant Cleland reporting as ordered, sir."

"Glad to meet you, Lieutenant. Have a seat." The general smiled.

Brigadier General Tom Rienzi—or "Big Tom," as his friends called him—stood six feet, six inches. He had played tackle on the West Point football team in 1942 and looked as if he could easily handle the same position now. Even sitting down he dwarfed me. His jump wings glistened, and his Legion of Merit ribbon stuck out proudly on his chest. When he turned to pick up my records, I noted his shoulder patch from the World War II China-Burma-India theatre.

General Rienzi liked the idea that I had trained in Washington, D.C., and had worked on a master's degree. I was awed and fascinated by this man who appeared to know what he wanted and how to get it. As I saluted and made my exit, I had the feeling that he wanted to work with me. I began to feel that I wanted to work with him, too.

The next day word came. I was to be the new aide-de-camp to the commanding general of the U.S. Army Signal Center and School. My orders to Vietnam were cancelled. He agreed, however, that after a year of working as his aide I could still go to Vietnam if I wished.

Tom Rienzi had been given the mission of putting the signal school on a wartime footing. Men waking up to answer early morning latrine calls would blink to see Big Tom out on predawn jogs, trailed by his tired aide. I logged miles of running each day to keep up with his hectic working schedule.

By the end of 1966 the signal school at Fort Monmouth was turning out hundreds of signal graduates each week trained in skills ranging from telephone line work to computer repair.

Along with this, General Rienzi ran a full-scale information program for foreign military dignitaries and Pentagon officials.

Dust billowed constantly from helicopters alighting on the parade ground next to the general's headquarters. Part of my job was to whisk VIPs to his office for a briefing, take them on a quick tour of the classrooms and the signal school's museum, give them lunch, and then put them back on their helicopter.

It was a fascinating, storybook job filled with new acquaintances, travel, challenge, and adventure. I could also enjoy an active social life, dating girls including some I'd met in Washington, D.C., and making new acquaintances in the Northeast.

But there was still a restlessness inside me. And I kept thinking of that other place where I'd rather be.

Vietnam.

Each day I reviewed the reasons why I felt I could not avoid the war of my generation. The drive for adventure was always prodding me. And I believed strongly in the grand tradition of America sticking up for its allies when they came under attack by aggressors.

But my idealism went beyond this. Men less trained, less motivated and younger than I, were being drafted and sent to Vietnam every day to die or get wounded. Deep within, I knew I could never be satisfied with myself if I hid behind a mahogany desk.

Finally, after months of agonizing, I decided that I had to go. General Rienzi heard me out and was silent for a moment, his head shaking ever so slightly.

What is he thinking? I wondered, watching his face closely.

He started to say something and thought better of it. "I made you a promise," he said. Then he called in a secretary and had orders cut for me to be assigned to the signal battalion with the First Cav.

My parents were crushed when I called them. Dad's voice choked, and Mother broke into tears. When I hung up the phone, I was sorry that I had hurt them. But I was finally going to do what I felt I was called to do. And mostly, what I wanted to do.

3

INTO ACTION

"It doesn't take courage to order men into battle.
It takes courage to go into battle."

— GENERAL H. NORMAN SCHWARZKOPF JR.

Our war chariot took off from San Francisco on May 31, 1967, with 272 young men aboard for the 23-hour flight to Saigon. The first stop was a landing in Hawaii for refueling. Next came Clark Field in the Philippines, and then we were off once more.

My bleary mind had completely lost any reference to American time when hours later the pilot's voice came over the loudspeaker. "If you look out the right side of the aircraft the coast of Vietnam is in sight."

I peered out the window. Vietnam looked like a soft green land rising out of a deep blue sea. *How deceptively tranquil*, I thought.

"Look!" Someone pointed to a plume of smoke rising from the jungle. There was excited speculation and talk of firefights and guerrilla raids.

As the plane descended we crossed over a patchwork of rice paddies before setting down on the runway at the Bien Hoa Air

Base outside of Saigon. I was startled to see swarms of Vietnamese men and women in big straw hats working on the airfield.

How many of them are infiltrators from the Viet Cong? The uncertainty that permeated this war was already beginning to build inside me in small ways.

Sweat immediately soaked through my uniform as I climbed down the ladder onto the pavement which shimmered in heat waves. A large group of tired-looking men in worn, bleached uniforms slumped on duffel bags nearby. Some wore crazy-looking hats. They had served their time in Vietnam and were on their way home. As I studied their drawn faces, I saw how eagerly they stared at our plane. What had been our war chariot was their freedom bird. It had also become a hearse. In the background, I could see stacks of shiny aluminum caskets ready for loading.

We were hustled into a nearby building where we changed into green jungle fatigues. These would be our uniforms from now on. Then we climbed into a U.S. Army bus for the trip to American headquarters at Long Binh. Heavy wire mesh covered the windows, protecting us from grenades that might be hurled at the open windows from the roadside. I looked again at the civilians outside, some walking, others on bicycles and motor scooters. A feeling crept over me, a feeling that would stick with me the rest of my time in Vietnam. It *was* an alien land.

The bus rumbled along the American-built highway, passing clusters of shacks. Pieced together from scrap metal, packing crates and even sheets of cardboard, these were homes for the Vietnamese. Smoke from cooking fires spiraled up from holes in the roofs, and ragged children played in the dust.

We rolled along beside a wooded area, and I saw in the distance what appeared to be a group of uniformed Boy Scouts led by a tall adult. As we neared them, I realized it was actually a

South Vietnamese Army squad led by an American Special Forces sergeant. The size difference was startling. It shook me. Somehow it symbolized for me, as could nothing else, the American burden in the war.

After processing at Long Binh, I was flown north in a C-130 cargo plane to the First Air Cavalry Division base camp in the central highlands. On climbing out of the plane, I looked up to see the big, horsehead emblem of the First Cav emblazoned on a mountainside looming behind the base. I had finally made it!

I was assigned as a platoon leader with the signal battalion. With 50 men and several million dollars worth of mobile signal equipment, we were to help provide around-the-clock communications for our division's logistics operation. This included installing telephone lines and switchboards and maintaining teletype and radio transmitters. First Cav radio teams were scattered all over Vietnam to handle classified messages for our 15,000-man division, including supply requests for everything from ammunition and chopper fuel to tents and lumber.

By midsummer of 1967, life at base camp had settled into a fairly dull routine. The greatest threat to our lifestyle came from voracious, biting insects and constant skin rashes from the hot, muggy, jungle atmosphere. After three months in Vietnam I began to feel like a veteran. But it didn't seem like much of a war.

While in the Danang area on a mission in late fall, I decided to visit a friend stationed there. Danang was a popular spot for American troops. There were round-eyed, Red Cross girls from the States, ice cream and steak from the Air Force, and all the liquor you could drink at the Navy officers' club. I loved dancing with the American girls and played the swashbuckling warrior role, brandishing the big, Cav horsehead patch on my shoulder. After a few hours, I set off to see the man I was looking for.

Hamilton McDonald—or Hammy as I called him—was an

American advisor to the Vietnamese headquarters. Two years ahead of me at Lithonia High, I remembered Hammy as a talented, dedicated young man. He had gone to North Georgia Military Academy, gotten a regular Army commission, gone to jump school, and then served as an Army captain in Germany.

In an office off a small courtyard, I found my friend's desk. His name, CPT. Hamilton McDonald, was written on the small marker. Someone said he had gone to lunch, and I decided to wait. As I sat beside his desk, I noticed a letter which Hammy had evidently just written, signed and left lying open, face up. Something caught my eye, and I found myself reading it in astonishment. It was his resignation from the Army. I could hardly believe it. Hammy was a career officer.

Footsteps sounded in the courtyard, and I turned to see Hammy striding toward the office. "Hammy!" I raised my hand in greeting.

At first he said nothing. His face was a grim mask as he stared at me. Then he said sharply, "Max, I think we're on the wrong side in this war."

I was dumbfounded. Neither of us spoke for a moment as we avoided each other's eyes.

Then Hammy laughed. "So what! Let's sit down and talk."

He relaxed somewhat and soon it was like old times as we caught each other up on college and military activities.

Then he grew sober again. "The Vietnamese just aren't hacking it," he said. He pointed around to empty Vietnamese desks. "We're supposed to be fighting a war and everyone's on a two-hour lunch break."

He told me about reconnoitering the area north of Danang in a small plane and discovering a large buildup of North Vietnamese forces. "I reported it here, but no one pays any attention," he said.

Shortly after our visit, Hammy's intelligence was confirmed

by other reconnaissance units. Our division was repositioned to
defend against a possible attack near Hue, but few believed the
enemy could mount a major offensive against us.

The Tet offensive exploded our complacency.

February 1, 1968, marked the beginning of the Chinese
New Year, Tet, the Year of the Monkey. On this date a horde of
North Vietnamese forces swept across the border like a tidal
wave. Firefights with U.S. troops broke out all through South
Vietnam. Many South Vietnamese units on pass for the holidays
simply disappeared.

Our division was hard hit. An Khe, the old First Cav
headquarters, had been mortared and the helicopter division's
air traffic control tower knocked out. Highway One, the main
road that went up the South Vietnamese coastline, was cut, and
the city of Hue was under siege. Both Marine and First Cav
forces were stranded outside the city and facing troops from
three North Vietnamese Army divisions. Casualties among our
infantry units were high.

How we survived the month of February I'll never know.
The monsoon rains were incessant, taking away much of the
Cav's helicopter mobility. Supplies ran dangerously low. Rocket
attacks were ever present, and the enemy pressure was intense.

But by the end of the month, the siege at Hue had broken.
The monsoon rains slackened, too, and we saw the sun for a few
days. As the enemy offensive eased, attention shifted to the one
spot still under serious threat—a little outpost in the north-
western corner of the country called Khe Sanh.

To the American public watching the drama unfold on their
television screens, Khe Sanh underscored America's precarious
position in the war. It was sudden and startling. Some knowl-
edgeable military advisors favored a strategic withdrawal, but
the top generals and President Johnson announced a joint decision that Khe Sanh would be held.

My adrenalin rose when I learned that the First Cav would form the nucleus of a secret, combined Army-marine operation to relieve the siege. Code-named *Pegasus*, the hope was that the flying helicopter horses of our special division would get to the besieged outpost in time and save it.

It looked like Khe Sanh would make history, and I wanted to be there. I had battled to get to Vietnam and now after nine months of not seeing any real action, I was itching to go to the main crisis point.

Again I felt compelled to volunteer.

I headed toward the tent of our signal battalion commander who had promoted me to captain only a few days before. Stepping into the colonel's tent, I saluted.

"Colonel, may I speak with you for a moment, sir?"

"Sit down, Captain Cleland," he said. "What's on your mind?"

"I'd like to volunteer to go with an infantry battalion as their communications officer, sir."

He shot me a quizzical look. "What do you want," he snapped, "a Purple Heart?"

"No, sir," I stammered, a little deflated by his lack of encouragement. "I'd just like to get some experience at the infantry level, sir."

The colonel walked over to a large wall map and pointed to one section. "You know it's all going to hit the fan at Khe Sanh?"

"Yes, sir."

"You know they kill people out there?" the colonel continued.

"I know that, sir."

The colonel shrugged. "Okay, Captain, if that's what you want."

As I left his tent I was stalked by the eerie feeling that I was now pushing myself to the outer limits of common sense.

A few days later just at dusk I visited my company commander, Captain Mike Barry, to say good-bye.

I particularly admired Mike. West Point all the way, he had punched his ticket in every combat school the Army had: paratroopers, rangers, pathfinders. He had even spent his first tour in Vietnam with the special forces. Now he was back on his second tour. I proudly told him that I was going to the Second Infantry Battalion of the Twelfth Cavalry with the Cav's second brigade.

"Well," he said, leaning back in his chair, hands behind his head, "you're in the plan then."

My heart leaped. "You mean to relieve Khe Sanh?"

"Yes," he said. "Two brigades will be air assaulted into the Khe Sanh area. Your brigade and the third brigade will be the lead elements."

A chill came over me. Had I heard him right? There were three North Vietnamese divisions out there. "You mean just *two* brigades?" I croaked. "How can we save them with just two brigades?"

Captain Barry tried to reassure me. "There'll be a South Vietnamese division to the south and a marine regiment attacking down Highway Nine."

I stared at him in disbelief. Such a pitifully small rescue force seemed almost suicidal. "The Marines can't get down that road because it's too chewed up and the South Vietnamese won't fight. What will happen to us if they don't make it?"

"That's the plan," said Barry impassively. He put his hand on my shoulder. "Look, Max, no U.S. Infantry company has been overrun in this whole war, much less two brigades."

"But we'll be dropped right into the middle of them," I argued, with a sudden feeling of sick desperation.

"That's right. With air support."

I turned from Barry's desk and stepped to the door of his tent. In the misty gloom I could see shadowy bunkers, tents, trucks, and choppers, all the equipment that makes up a division. *My*

God, we are really going in there. Gripped with fear, I wiped my forehead.

What was happening to me? I had wanted to put myself to the ultimate test. Now that it had come I was weak with fear. Even more chilling was the realization that with less than 90 days of my Vietnam tour to go, I had deliberately forced myself into this predicament. I felt sick over my stupidity.

When I arrived by jeep at the headquarters of my new battalion, I was quickly led to the "old sarge" of the signal unit. He regarded me with undisguised contempt. While he and his small unit had lived through the toughest part of the war, he had borne the brunt of leadership alone. Now he did not relish having some signal officer arrive to tell him what to do.

As we were due to launch our attack at the beginning of April, only four weeks away, I asked him how ready our communications were.

"They're not," he grunted. "Radios are on the blink, the generators need repair, and if you can find me a decent antenna around here I'll eat it."

I managed to scrounge enough replacement parts to start the generators working and get the battalion's radios back on the air. But meanwhile my fear over our rescue mission grew. In a letter to an aunt I confessed my worries: "If I ever make it back to the Atlanta airport, I'll be happy just to crawl home regardless of what shape I'm in."

All my bravado was slipping away. First, I tried to get my old signal battalion commander to reverse my orders that brought me to this danger spot. The orders stood.

Then I went to our battalion executive officer, Major Maury Crallé, and confessed, "I'm just not sure how I'll measure up when we go into action."

Major Crallé smiled. "Max," he said, "congratulations on being normal. Just keep your mind on your job, and you'll do fine."

His confidence bolstered me—somewhat. But fear continued to eat at my innards.

As the first of April approached, the tension grew in our battalion. One Sunday, I decided to attend an outdoor chapel service. We sat on benches just as I had as a boy in the small, rural church outside Lithonia. Only this time there were no revival hymns and no altar call. Instead, there was a low-key message about faith and trust. I needed help with my fears, but I did not get "foxhole religion."

I made a conscious decision to depend on my own skills and ability. I would stick with that.

At dawn on April 1, 1968, the First Air Cavalry Division launched its biggest air assault of the war. In the thunder of a hundred helicopter engines, the third brigade led the way, blackening the sky as the choppers charged, nose-down, toward Khe Sanh.

Our brigade was poised to follow the next morning, making our assault landing on a small ridge in the mountain range east of Khe Sanh.

But when D-day arrived, trouble struck. The radio in the battalion commander's helicopter went stone dead.

Radio communication was vital. The Cav's air mobility and artillery support were helpless if the battalion commander could not communicate with his troops or coordinate artillery preparations on the landing zone.

There was no time to get it fixed since our choppers were already lifting off. I tried to think fast.

"Another headset will do it," came a shout above the helicopter roar.

We found an extra headset and jumped into a jeep. Then we careened down toward a big Chinook, its blades spinning in a blur as it lifted off. The jeep skidded to a stop in a billow of dust. I leaped out and dashed for the helicopter which was already about 10 feet off the ground. The pilot saw me and held the ship as I flung the headset into its open tail door. "Give 'em to the colonel," I shouted as loud as I could into the dust and prop wash.

As the Chinook lifted into the morning mist, I slumped back onto the jeep hood like I had just dodged a bullet. *What would the president think if he knew this war was being fought on a shoestring?*

On April 3, my signal team and I filled a chopper as we headed for the landing zone near Khe Sanh which the battalion had secured. None of us said much as the giant Chinook thundered on, its slipstream blast whipping our fatigues as we hunched on the metal seats. I glanced at our "old sarge," looking as calm as if he'd gone through this a dozen times before— which he had. I could only guess at how I would handle myself.

As soon as we touched ground, I leaped from the ship and raced for cover, certain that we would soon be fired at. Then I stopped in mid-stride and looked around in astonishment. From our position I gazed two miles down into a valley at the Khe Sanh outpost. Every inch of ground between us had been pulverized by bombs dropped by our B-52s. What was once jungle was now a wasteland, nothing but countless bomb craters. It looked like the surface of the moon—and just as dead.

I breathed easier. Suddenly Khe Sanh didn't seem so fearsome after all. My heart pounded in a strange mixture of fear and joy.

At the center of our landing zone yawned a deep bomb crater some 20 feet in diameter. I positioned my signal team inside it.

Since the enemy could reach us with artillery fire, we all worked feverishly, sweating through our uniforms under the hot midday sun as we lugged power generators, radios, antennas, and backup equipment into the pit which still reeked of explosives.

The next day at about dusk, I was half inside my makeshift foxhole in the bomb crater holding a flashlight in one hand and trying to write a letter when a screaming whistle and explosion split the air.

"Incoming," someone shouted. "Take cover."

Another deafening explosion shook the earth again as the second artillery round struck, and I found myself flat on my face, dirt gritting in my teeth. The air was split by screams of incoming rounds and a rapid cadence of thunderous blasts. Mixed with it were the cries of wounded men and the hoarse shouting of orders. Suddenly it was all over. I huddled in my foxhole waiting. Then "old sarge's" voice roared: "Take care of the wounded. Prepare for a ground attack."

Someone passed around a wooden crate with hand grenades in it and everybody took two apiece. Standard procedure was to bend back the ends of the pin so that the pin could not slip out by accident. The pin would actually have to be yanked out to make the grenade live. In the growing darkness, I bent the ends back as best I could, then hooked the grenades onto the belt webbing across my chest.

Picking up my M-16, I crawled to the lip of the crater and peered through the smoke and deepening night down toward Khe Sanh. *How many of the enemy are out there? Are they creeping up the hill now? Can they take us?* My hands trembled on the trigger of my M-16 as doubts and fears rang through my head.

Suddenly, thunderous explosions split the twilight and the ground heaved. I ducked back into the crater and then realized something. It was *our* artillery. In the distance I could see the bright yellow explosions of our hits piercing the black, brooding valley.

I'm not sure how long our attack lasted. The night became a blur of explosions and screams. Soon, a gray light dawned exposing the grisly horror of what artillery could do. Four of our men lay dead. A number of wounded waited on stretchers for medevac choppers. Some moaned almost breathlessly, others cried out, some lay quietly staring at the sky. A tremor of cold went through me as I looked at one of the dead. There was little left of him below the knees—just blood-soaked fragments of green fatigues. A white shin bone jutted out in splinters in the early morning sunlight. I shuddered and turned away.

On April 5, infantry units of our battalion left our hilltop landing zone and moved toward the Khe Sanh base. During the next three days, they secured the intermediate hills and advanced closer to the Khe Sanh perimeter. During that first week of April, our infantry companies joined the U.S. Marine forces and elements of the Cav's third brigade to help break the longest, most spectacular siege of the Vietnam War.

It was a spectacular rescue mission in which U.S. forces used hundreds of planes, thousands of troops, and millions of pounds of firepower. But two weeks after the siege was broken, the Khe Sanh bunkers which had been so carefully constructed, the cargo plane runway which had proved a lifeline for the besieged, and the gas drums which had held precious fuel were all plowed under by U.S. Army bulldozers.

Then the entire base was abandoned.

Breaking the siege of Khe Sanh had no lasting value because a bigger game for larger stakes was being played out on the television screens of Americans who saw in the Tet offensive and the siege of Khe Sanh not success but defeat. As one writer noted: "The war reached the peak of absurdity, and from that moment on it was lost."

4

THE GREAT DEATH

"Courage is doing your job while you're half scared to death."

— GENERAL OMAR BRADLEY

Long before dawn on April 8, I was awake. As I gazed down at the flickering lights of the Khe Sanh base, now quiet in an eerie sort of way, the horizon blushed pink and suddenly a great orange sun lifted into the sky. Exhilaration filled me. I thought of Kipling's words about the dawn coming up "like thunder out of China 'crost the bay."

This beautiful April morning signaled the ending of the monsoon rains. Now time and weather were on our side. The air was quiet, disturbed only by the morning mutter of men.

I stood on the edge of our bomb crater that had been my home for five days and five nights, stretched my six-foot, two-inch frame and was caught up in excitement. The battle for Khe Sanh was over, and I had come out of it unhurt and alive! Five terrible days and nights were behind us.

The sun was now blindingly bright as I squinted down the valley, laughing at my apprehensions. In spite of the dire predictions, we had held Khe Sanh. I had scored a personal victory over myself and my fears. I had become a soldier and could really look the old sarge in the face. As Stephen Crane stated in his great book on war, *The Red Badge of Courage*, "I went to face the Great Death and found it was only the Great Death."

My tour of duty in Vietnam was now almost over. In another month I'd be going home. I smiled, thinking of the good times waiting stateside.

"Oh, Captain Cleland."

I looked around. It was Major Crallé who had come up to our position. "The battalion needs a better radio hookup with the division supply area," he said. "I'd like you to send a radio relay team back there to improve communications."

That meant setting up a radio relay station on a hill back at the division forward assembly area 15 miles to the east. Instead of sending a team alone, I decided to go with them to ensure they got set up properly.

With two men, I pulled together some antennas and a generator and some radios and loaded them on a chopper. The three of us climbed in and the helicopter lifted off. Within minutes, we had settled down by the radio relay station. The men and equipment were unloaded, and I climbed back into the chopper intending to go down to battalion rear headquarters.

Then two ideas crossed my mind. First, it would be better to work personally with my team in setting up the radio relay. Second, I had a lot of friends at this relay station and now was a good time to have a cold beer with them.

I called to the pilot that I was getting out. He nodded and held the ship steady. I jumped to the ground, ran in a crouch until I got clear of the spinning helicopter blades, turned around and watched the chopper lift.

Then I saw the grenade. It was where the chopper had lifted off.

It must be mine, I thought. Grenades had fallen off my web gear before. Shifting the M-16 to my left hand and holding it behind me, I bent down to pick up the grenade.

A blinding explosion threw me backwards.

The blast jammed my eyeballs back into my skull, temporarily blinding me, pinning my cheeks and jaw muscles to the bones of my face. My ears rang with a deafening reverberation as if I were standing in an echo chamber.

Memory of the firecracker exploding in my hand as a child flashed before me.

When my eyes cleared I looked at my right hand. It was gone. Nothing but a splintered white bone protruded from my shredded elbow. It was speckled with fragments of bloody flesh. Nausea flooded me. I lay where the blast had flung me for a moment, fighting for breath. I found myself slumped on the ground.

Then I tried to stand but couldn't. I looked down. My right leg and knee were gone. My left leg was a soggy mass of bloody flesh mixed with green fatigue cloth. The combat boot dangled awkwardly, like the smashed legs on the dead soldier after the rocket attack.

What was left of me? I reached with my left hand to feel my head. My steel helmet—now gone—had apparently protected it. My flak jacket had shielded my chest and groin from shrapnel.

Intense pain throbbed my body with each heartbeat. I seemed to be falling backwards into a dark tunnel.

I raised up on my left elbow to call for help. Apparently, surrounding troops had mistaken the blast for incoming rocket fire and frantically scattered. I tried to cry out to them but could only hiss. My hand touched my throat and came back covered with blood. Shrapnel had sliced open my windpipe.

I sank back on the ground knowing that I was dying fast. A soft blackness was trying to claim me. *No! I don't want to die.* The words burned through my head. I fought to stay alert to what was going on around me. If I gave in now, I knew I would never regain consciousness.

"Somebody call a medic!" screamed a GI. The men slowly emerged from hiding. "Get a medevac in here—right now!" someone barked.

Men stood over me, their faces white. One began cutting off my fatigues. I felt naked having my uniform ripped off in such an unceremonious fashion. I clung to consciousness as they worked.

"Hold on there, Captain," said a young man as he carefully wrapped my arm stump with his T-shirt. "The chopper will be here in a minute."

Time seemed suspended. Powerful waves of pain now surged through my body. Every fibre of me seemed to be on fire. I couldn't look into the men's faces as they worked feverishly over me. I stared into the clear blue sky that I had welcomed so gratefully that morning. One aching thought spun through my head: *God, why me?*

A familiar roar tremored the ground. Prop blast from the incoming medevac chopper billowed dust into my face.

Two medics leaped out with a stretcher and helped ease me onto it. I was lifted into the helicopter. As the engine roared into takeoff, someone yelled, "You're going to make it, Captain. You'll be okay."

I tried to answer but could only hiss the words through my cut windpipe. "Hell, yes, I'm going to make it."

As I lay on the chopper floor, the pain flooding through me, I looked up at the medic as he stuck an IV needle into my left arm.

"Have I lost much blood?" I croaked.

"Well, not much, Captain," he said, steadily hooking the needle tube to a plasma bottle.

The chopper landed at the division aid station. I was hurried into a bunker and stretched out on a table where medics worked on me.

Someone asked: "Name? Rank? Service number?"

Is he serious? I'm dying, and this guy is asking me questions. Angry thoughts pounded in with the pain.

With all the defiance I could muster, I tried to shout. But I could barely whisper, "Cleland, Joseph M., captain, service number zero . . . five . . . three . . . two three . . . four three six."

Fear invaded me now. Every nerve cried out as I struggled to breathe. I shrank from looking at my mangled body. Instead, I stared up at one of the medics working on my arm stump with surgical scissors.

"What do you think?" I wheezed. "Am I going to make it?"

He continued snipping.

"You just might," he murmured, keeping his eyes on his work. He stuck a needle in my arm and pulled it out.

"What was that?"

"Morphine."

Suddenly, a familiar face appeared over me. It was Captain Barry. He was ashen. "What happened?" he asked softly.

I tried to tell him about the grenade. "It just blew up . . . it . . . just blew up."

The medics hurried me out to a waiting medevac chopper for a flight to a surgical hospital at Quang Tri, 40 miles to the east. All through the 24-minute flight I was conscious, trying to understand what happened, trying to make the chopper go faster. Lying flat on the floor, I thought about potential snipers below and that I had more of my body exposed than was necessary. Then I realized that snipers couldn't do much more to me than already had been done.

At Quang Tri, attendants at the 38th Surgical Field Hospital rushed to the chopper, grabbed the stretcher and, hunching under the blades, whisked me into the surgical quonset hut where I was lifted onto a litter bed. They rolled the bed directly into the operating room where a team of four doctors began working on me immediately.

I tried to concentrate on their low voices. "He's bleeding badly now," said one. I learned later that flash burns from the exploding grenade had seared my flesh, slowing the immediate bleeding. But now the wounds were hemorrhaging freely.

I fought the drowsiness that was overtaking me. I knew I might not make it back. I was also choking, and I pointed to my throat. A doctor grabbed my slit windpipe and held it open with his finger so I could get more air. He said they would perform a tracheotomy so I could breathe better.

"Please save my leg," I gasped to another physician.

"We'll do all we can," he said reassuringly.

I seemed to be sinking down and down into a dark, deep vortex as the anesthesia took over. My last thought was amazement at how many limbs I had lost in so short a time.

Groggily, I tried to make sense of my surroundings. I was in a bed somewhere, and I could dimly sense the presence of another person sitting nearby.

Time passed and then I was able to comprehend that the person was a girl—a young girl. She was either a nurse or a Red Cross volunteer, I couldn't tell which.

I tried to speak but could hardly make a sound. She looked up and stepped over to the bed.

"Have—have I got my leg?" I whispered.

Her eyes moistened. "No," she said softly.

Oh my God! Both legs gone! I wanted to bury my face in the pillow but couldn't move. I lay there for a while looking into her stricken face. Pain still pounded through me. How much else was gone? At first I was afraid to look.

Then, unable to raise my head to see, I tried to move my left arm. But it bristled with so many IV needles that I could hardly budge it. Then I tried to flex my leg muscles.

Nothing happened on the left one, but I felt something on the right! My spirits surged. I could move a muscle in my right leg—the muscle that I knew controlled my knee.

"I've got my right knee," I whispered excitedly.

She shook her head sadly.

"I'm sure," I argued. "I can move it a little."

She put a cool hand on my forehead. "It's only the muscle," she whispered. "Now try to get some sleep."

Her face wavered through my tears. I didn't even have a knee left. I lay there staring at the ceiling.

Then I noticed my right arm in a sling. The forearm and hand were gone. She saw me looking at it and volunteered in a small, quiet voice, "It's kinda like traction. It works to pull the flesh down over the elbow bone so the end can heal."

She told me that I had been in the operating room for more than five hours the day before. They had given me 41 pints of blood. "You can thank God," she added softly. "It's a miracle you're alive."

I shut my eyes and winced. *Thanks for nothing*, I thought.

I looked up at her again. "I'll get artificial limbs, won't I?"

"Sure," she said soothingly. "They'll fix you up."

I tried to drift off into sleep to escape the pain and misery of knowing what had happened to me. But I could not. My body seemed aflame with fever.

"Water," I whispered.

The girl bent over me, her eyes pained, and said that I couldn't have anything to drink. I didn't realize that my body fluids were being carefully monitored and controlled and that if I took any extra liquids it would flush the remaining vital fluids from my body. I continued to plead for water.

Finally, she moistened a small piece of cotton and put it on my cracked lips. I sucked the cotton, then begged for more.

She shook her head. I thought of all the iced tea and lemonade I used to have at home. Still working on the dry cotton, I finally slipped into unconsciousness.

It was sometime the next day when I woke up. I was told I was going to the naval hospital in Danang for an overnight stop, then to an Army field hospital further south. I slipped in and out of consciousness as I moved from plane to plane. After a trip in a C-130 cargo plane down the coast, a helicopter transferred me to a small Army hospital in the Vietnamese village of Thuy Hoa.

It was little more than a hut—and it was steaming hot. Two small air-conditioning units vibrated vainly against the heat. And the stench was almost unbearable. There were about 30 patients in the hut. I was the only American. The intensive care unit was used for both allied and enemy casualties. On my left was a silent North Vietnamese prisoner, to my right a glaze-eyed Viet Cong.

At night, the hut temperatures plummeted to an icy cold. The swing in temperatures raised my continuing fever. At 4 A.M., following my arrival, the attendants decided to try to bring it under control with an alcohol rubdown. Convulsing with chills, I thought I was about to die.

Morning brought a little relief in the form of fresh air. This was possible only during the cool, early dawn hours when the end doors were opened for a few minutes to dilute the stench.

None of the pain I experienced was as intense as when a doctor decided to change all my dressings at the same time shortly after my arrival. Just touching the bandages sent agony flooding through me. Both thighs were as open as a slab of raw beef and my arm still had the bone sticking out of it. After a shot of Demerol, the doctor pulled away the blood-encrusted bandages one after another. It reminded me of a movie I had once seen when a cowboy was given a bullet to bite and a slug of whisky while his trusty buddy amputated his leg.

Despite my continued agony and the frequent drifting in and out of consciousness, I soon realized how strange this hospital was. The medical staff walked around like zombies and seemed far removed from what they were doing. Then I began to understand why. They had become casualties of the war just as we had. After breathing blood and death for months, they were victims of "psychic numbing."

It had particularly affected one of the day-shift nurses. One morning I had been helped painfully onto the bedpan by an attendant. But he was gone, and I was ready to get off.

The day-shift nurse was with another patient across the ward. I called to her for help.

"Do it yourself," she shouted angrily. "I'm busy."

Supporting myself with my left arm, I somehow inched off the pan.

By Easter Sunday, April 14, 1968, the infection in my body was full blown. Six days had passed since the accident but my legs and arm stumps were still raw and open. My lungs were filling with fluid, and my windpipe had to be suctioned every few hours to keep the fluid from drowning me. When my fever reached 102 degrees, I felt that either it would break or I would die in this miserable hut.

When a Vietnamese nursing aide took my blood pressure, he was alarmed that it had dropped so low and reported this to the physician on duty. An order was placed for blood plasma.

Unfortunately, the nurse I had shouted at from the bedpan was responsible for setting up my IV feeding. Through an oversight she failed to turn on the mechanism that would allow the plasma to drain into me when she left to attend another patient. Burning with fever and my strength ebbing fast, I called out to her: "Come over here and turn this damned thing on."

Her head shot up and she wheeled on me: "Shut up and take a tranquilizer."

"The hell I'll take a tranquilizer," I spat. With low blood pressure and fever, I didn't think I could stand one.

The nurse stood, hands on hips, and froze me with one of her looks.

I fell back on my pillow and reached for the tranquilizer. Someone eventually turned on the IV feeder, but my fever soared higher. Other attendants aimed electric fans at me. Finally, they gave me an aspirin.

I floated in and out of consciousness throughout the nightmarish experience. Desperately grasping for something to hold onto, I fantasized a congressional investigation into this hospital. *I'll have this whole hospital blown right off the map,* I dreamed.

After a week I began to reason more clearly and thought of calling Mom and Dad. I knew by now they had received the standard telegram sent to families of the wounded *(The Secretary of the Army has asked me to inform you . . .)* telling them I was on the "seriously ill" list.

As yet, I did not want them to know my real condition. But I had to talk to them.

It was a weird conversation. Using a regular overseas telephone in this little, outpost hospital was out of the question. But thanks to a radio patch hookup through MARS (Military Affiliate Radio Station), manned by a volunteer ham operator in California, I reached home.

Though still foggy under the Demerol, I was thrilled to hear Mom in the receiver which they brought to my bed.

"Mother, this is Max. Over."

Each statement had to end with "over" so the shortwave operator could switch his transmitter to the other person.

"Hello, Max. How are you? Over."

"Fine, Mom. I hope to be seeing you and Dad soon. Over."

Back and forth it went. A crackling hum filled the airways as our voices traveled 12,000 miles. But thanks to some unknown person on the West Coast of the United States, a son could tell his family he would soon be coming home.

5

POLAR ROUTE
HOME

*"For those who fight for it, life has a flavor
the protected never know."*

— FOUND ON A U.S. MARINE BUNKER AT
KHE SANH, VIETNAM, 1968

Some good news at last! I was going to an Army hospital in
Japan. Seven days in the Thuy Hoa field had seemed like an
eternity.

By the time my stretcher was lifted onto the big Air Force
C-130, I could hardly remember the name of the nurse I had
battled or much about the hospital itself. Everything disappeared in a fog of pain and Demerol.

My spirits lifted a fraction. Now I just might get out of
Vietnam alive. If I could make it out of here, I reasoned, I could
make it anywhere.

The C-130 landed near Yokohama, Japan. The rear door
went down and I, along with the other stretcher cases, was put
on a hospital bus headed for the 106th General Army Hospital
just outside the city. As we rolled along, I tried to raise myself
up a little to look out the window. I had never seen Japan. But
since I could barely move my head, I lay there staring at the tiny

holes on the bus' sound-absorbent ceiling.

At the big Army hospital, I was quickly moved to surgery. In the operating room, the doctors finally closed my leg stumps and my throat "trache." Since the six-inch gash on my right arm stump had not healed enough to close over the exposed bone, it was left open to drain. I soon discovered that the 106th General Army was a superior hospital in every way, with nurses and ward attendants who cared for us with true compassion.

Within a few days I awoke sensing a new spirit within me. The blue sky outside the ward-room window seemed especially bright, a nurse hurrying by my bed threw me a cheery hello, and I found myself responding with a grin and a wave. Somehow I had managed to turn the corner. I *knew* that I was going to live.

Meanwhile I was trying to adjust to my new shape. When a nurse taking my blood pressure would place the instrument case on the lower part of my bed, I would instinctively draw back my "legs." And those first mornings when I woke up, I would try to throw my legs over the side of the bed to walk to the latrine.

I also tried to adjust to my new surroundings and take more interest in my fellow patients. One of them mentioned the terrific bargains to be had in stereo equipment in the U.S. Navy PX in Tokyo.

Good stereo equipment had always interested me. One day I asked a young ward sergeant, "Hey, how far is it to Tokyo? I'm interested in some of those stereo buys I hear they have over there."

He laughed. "Sounds like you're getting better, Captain." Then he thought for a moment. "I'll do you one better. I'm heading that way myself. How about my ordering it for you?"

"That's great," I replied. Then I outlined what I wanted in the way of speakers, turntable, and receiver.

When he returned, he reported that he was able to get

everything and have the equipment shipped to my home in Lithonia.

The price was $824. I was elated. It would have cost three times that much in the States.

Then a thought struck me. Though I had money in the bank, I had no funds with me. "How will I pay for it?" I asked.

"Oh," he said, "they'll take a check."

But how was I going to write a check? I had been right-handed. From now on I'd have to do everything with my left.

The sergeant took a check from my wallet, filled out the amount, and handed it to me along with a pen.

I laid the check down on a lap board and slowly scrawled my name on it. It looked very much like the way I had written it in the second grade.

I handed it to him and laughed: "With a signature like that it'll bounce."

He grinned. "Nah, it won't. No forger would ever write a signature that poorly."

That day I dictated a letter to Mom and Dad with the help of a Red Cross volunteer. I didn't tell them everything, just that I was doing okay and would call them when I got to Walter Reed Army Hospital in Washington, D.C.

The word had come through that this hospital would be my next stop.

As the days passed, flashbacks of the grenade explosion began to haunt me. I replayed the incident over and over like a video-tape. The memories were vivid and painful. I'd run under the chopper blades, watch the helicopter lift, then look down. The grenade. Explosion.

Again and again I analyzed the scene in every detail, try-ing desperately to change the ending. Whose grenade was it?

How did the pin come out? I didn't know for sure, but each time I ended up with the same feeling. Somehow *I* had fumbled the ball.

One minute I would be utterly grateful that I was still able to see, breathe, feel, and think. The next minute I would sink into despair knowing that I would never again walk on my own legs, that I would never again be the man I once was, that I would never again be like other people.

As time passed, I began to question myself. Why had I volunteered so persistently to go to Vietnam? Why had I pressed my luck? What was I trying to prove?

My signal battalion commander's face floated before me as he asked, "What do you want, a Purple Heart?"

No, I had said. But in my heart the answer was *yes*. For some reason I had wanted my own red badge of courage.

But even now I had not found it. My 11 months in Vietnam had proved little. Virtually everything about it had been disillusioning. Though wounded, I was just another grim casualty in a frustrating war. Even the climactic struggle at Khe Sanh seemed meaningless. I had more and more questions about the war, my life, and my future—and fewer and fewer answers.

A hospital bus was taking a load of us patients to the airfield. From there we would be airlifted to the States. As we rumbled along through suburban Yokohama, this time I did manage to raise up on my good elbow. Yokohama was the last slice of Asia that I would see, and I felt a strange sense of regret at being unable to get to know it better.

On a stretcher next to me on the bus was another triple-amputee, hardly more than a teenager. He had lost both arms and one leg. The boy's thin body was lost under the sheet, and his hollow eyes stared skull-like at the ceiling. A corpsman kneeled next to him holding a Coke with a straw through which the youngster sucked desperately. For the first time I felt almost fortunate.

"How ya makin' it?" I asked.

He rolled big, round, sunken eyes at me. "I'm hot," he gasped. "It's hot in here."

"I know what you mean," I said. I continued watching him, thinking, *Poor kid.*

As I felt the bus slow down and enter the airfield, I became uneasy. I was leaving the protective environment of the hospital. I was leaving good friends, especially nurses and ward attendants who had cared for me well through rough days.

Men began unloading our stretchers. Suddenly, I did not want to leave. I didn't want to face my family and friends. I wanted to stay here where I had forever left a good part of myself.

The corpsmen hustled my stretcher up the rear, cargo ramp of the big Lockheed C-141 Air Force hospital ship and placed it in a steel frame. The locks snapped into place. I lay flat on my back, naked under my sheet. My right arm with its six-inch, unhealed gash was held high above me in traction. And now I suffered from an overwhelming urge to urinate. Just before I had left the hospital they had removed the catheter tube which had drained my bladder for 16 days. I had tried to relieve myself before we left but couldn't. I didn't know I'd developed a slight muscular blockage in my urinary tract.

The jet engines roared, and my left hand gripped the stretcher rail as our ship rumbled down the runway and lifted from the Yokohama airstrip. After 331 days in Asia, I was finally returning home.

The slim form of an Air Force nurse passed beside me and I asked her what route we'd take to the States.

"The polar route," she said. "It's faster. It'll only take us about 16 hours."

As our ship climbed into the Pacific sky, there was little talk from the hundred or so casualties and only an occasional word from a nurse or corpsman. Most of the men slept.

Hours passed. The light outside the portholes dimmed only slightly. I tried to imagine the land and sea beneath us. *We really are going over the top of the world.* The constant light created a sense of unreality, and I felt lost in space. I yearned for the relief of darkness.

I also yearned for another kind of relief. The nurse gave me a urinal, but I could not use it, strain though I did.

A deep loneliness closed in on me. With the mesmerizing of jet engines, the plane seemed to be going nowhere. Flat on my back, helpless and in pain, I felt lost in some no-man's land.

I began to sob.

The young nurse stepped over, uncertain of what to do. Finally, she must have resorted to her psychology training. "How can I help you adjust?" she asked.

"I don't know," I sobbed. "I don't know." She seemed every bit as shaken as I was. Finally she stammered, "Can . . . can I get you some orange juice or something?"

"No!" I bawled loudly, knowing that a drink would only intensify my bladder pain. "Just give me a shot."

Mercifully she did so, and I drifted off into the drugdream world that I was coming to know and love.

The next thing I knew an icy blast of wind rippled my sheet. *Have we crashed in the Arctic Sea?* My thoughts were jumbled. In panic, I fought for full consciousness. Then shrill female voices at the rear of the plane began chanting, "Welcome home! Welcome home! Welcome back to the U.S.A.!"

"What the hell's going on?" I asked the nurse.

"We're in Anchorage, Alaska," she answered. "A refueling stop."

The crew had opened the tailgate to air the cabin. I shivered.

The female voices grew louder as a covey of overly cheerful women stormed through the plane, chattering greetings to the astonished men, giving them cookies and picture postcards of Anchorage. Clutching the sheet to my chin, I stared at them in dismay, wanting only privacy. As we left Alaska, I again dozed off.

I was awakened as the nurse flicked on the cabin lights. It was dark outside the portholes now. "We're almost there," she said, trying to be cheerful. "We're circling and about to make our final approach into Washington."

The 16-hour flight was over, and my unrelieved bladder felt like a huge ball of cement at the base of my gut.

When the wheels touched down on the runway at Andrews Air Force Base, everyone inside the plane was quiet—no cheers, no visible emotion, just silence. The orange and purple runway lights gleamed in the darkness as the tailgate opened. An odd thought played through my head. I noted that in Hawaii, the Philippines, Vietnam, Thailand, Malaysia, Japan and now in Washington, runway lights all looked the same.

There was no crowd waiting. As I was carried off the plane, I noticed a few people standing in the glow of the landing lights, anxiously searching our faces. They were obviously friends or relatives of some of the patients.

Suddenly, my sense of loneliness intensified. I wished I had told my parents to meet the plane.

"Captain Cleland?" a voice called out. I answered, relieved to hear the sound of my name in this strange environment.

It was an attendant. "We have an ambulance here to take you to Walter Reed."

Soon we were out of the downtown area of the capital and driving along the peaceful, tree-lined residential avenues of northwest Washington. Then the ambulance pulled up to the receiving entrance of Walter Reed Hospital. Its massive, red-brick structure towered over me as I was wheeled in on a litter bed.

The attendants pushed me to the hospital admission office where a volunteer met me, ready to make that phone call home the Red Cross gives a serviceman when he arrives back in the States.

It was late at night, but my mother answered on the second ring. She sounded relieved to know I was back in the country and in the care of Walter Reed. I talked with Dad, too, and they immediately began making plans to visit.

I couldn't talk long. My bladder was bursting, and I was in agony. I tried to reassure them and then hung up.

Exhausted and wincing from the pain, I was moved to a ward. A nurse greeted me and followed while the attendant wheeled me into a dimly lit enclave at the end of a corridor.

"Gentlemen," the nurse said, addressing the semi-darkness which was lit only by a few television sets, "this is Captain Cleland. He'll be with us for a while."

"Welcome to the 'snake pit,'" came a deep, rasping voice from the shadows.

6

THE SNAKE PIT

"Success is how high you bounce after you hit bottom."

— General George S. Patton Jr.

The deep voice rasped again after I was placed on a bed and the attendants and the nurse left.

"Hi, my name's Harry."

"I'm Max," I grunted as my eyes adjusted to the dim light. Turning my head to the left, I saw that Harry was a big, heavy-set man with dark, crewcut hair. He glanced at the lower part of my bed. "You got it pretty good."

I replied with a groan, "Man, I'm about to burst. I haven't taken a leak in 18 hours. What do I do?"

Suddenly, from down the hall came a clanging noise. It sounded like somebody was banging garbage can lids together like cymbals. A female aide in her early 20s with a plump, shapely figure under her white uniform walked in carrying a handful of aluminum urinals.

She shot Harry a disdainful glance and approached me. "You can probably use one of these," she drawled, placing one on my bedstand. She pivoted on her nurse's shoes and disappeared down the hall.

"That's Joanna," whispered Harry. "She's not only a WAC but a little bit wacky, too." He chuckled. "She tries hard, though. Takes pretty good care of us."

I was too busy adjusting the urinal to hear Harry's chatter. But to my dismay the muscular problem in my urinary tract still had me tied up. I began moaning in pain.

Suddenly a voice from the corner complained: "Who's making all that racket?"

"Take it easy, Major," Harry said. "We've got a new guy here, and he's having a little trouble making a tinkle."

In the gloom I could make out a tall thin man in his early 30s. As he swung himself out of bed, he seemed to have all his arms and legs.

"Can't tinkle, eh?" he said, walking to the end of my bed. "Well, that's too bad. Where'd they get you—in the pecker?"

"No, sir," I replied meekly. "For some reason I just can't go."

The major moved across the room to the bathroom. "Sometimes all it takes is a little reminding, you know," he called, as an unmistakable sound emerged. "Sometimes it's all in the mind. Just listen and concentrate."

He finished and came out of the bathroom. "How're you doing now?"

"Not good, sir," I gasped. "I need a doctor before I split."

Harry reached over to his table and pressed the call button. A nurse walked in, and I convinced her that I needed help.

The night doctor came next and quickly ordered a catheter. Then a corpsman arrived to perform the delicate task of inserting the long tube into my bladder through the urinary tract.

Relief! Soon I was able to relax for the first time since leaving Japan. Then the nurse gave me a sleeping pill and I drifted off.

"Mawnin', everybody!"

The high, shrill voice sounded like someone screeching chalk across a blackboard.

"How's ma lil' babies this mawnin'?"

Groans from the huddled masses in the beds acknowledged daybreak. Someone managed enough gallantry to reply, "Morning, Major Baker."

I looked up to see a thin woman in her early 50s stride purposefully into the ward. The crow's feet beside her dark eyes crinkled as she smiled. From the good-natured greetings by the guys, I could see that her personal warmth was much appreciated.

She stepped over to my bed, measuring my condition.

"Mornin', Cap'n Cleland. How you doin' this fine mornin'?" Perhaps it was the Southern drawl in her voice that made me a bit perky.

"Well, ma'am, my right arm is a bit of a problem—it's beginning to smell."

"The dressing needs changing," she said, motioning to a corpsman to fetch clean gauze. "You need a bath, too," she smiled, "but we can't put you in water just yet. We'll get you bathed in bed."

A bath! I hadn't even thought about one. The last shower I had was in Vietnam back in March. As for a tub bath, that had been almost four months ago in January at a hotel in Kuala Lumpur during a brief leave.

The next thing I knew Major Baker was attacking my bandages with scissors. I winced in apprehension and cautioned her, "That's my skin under there."

Major Baker slowly withdrew her scissors and gave me a long look. "Cap'n, how old are you?"

"I'm 25, ma'am."

"I was changing dressings and carrying out bedpans before you were born," she said calmly.

As she cut the bandages, she glanced at the dressings around the ends of my thigh stumps. "They'll want to change those, too. After we get you cleaned up this morning, you'll go on up to the cast room so the doctor can take a look at you."

"I'm not much to see," I said glumly.

She looked at me sharply. "Now, don't talk like that, Cap'n Cleland. You're a good-lookin' young man, and you are going to make it out of here just fine."

Her words boosted me. I decided to risk it and ask the important question. "How long, Major Baker? How long?"

She continued cleaning the gaping wound in my right arm stump and didn't reply for a moment. Then, keeping her eyes on her work, she replied matter-of-factly, "It'll take a while."

My spirit sagged. If someone like Major Baker couldn't give me a straight answer, I knew I was in for a tough time.

On the morning of April 27, 1968, my first day at Walter Reed, I was pushed on a litter bed down the hall and taken by elevator up to the cast room. It was now just three weeks after the grenade explosion. The cast room was brightly lighted and expansive, gleaming with stainless-steel fixtures, and bustling with activity. A dozen white-coated doctors and aides busily worked with patients. They changed dressings, studied the healing progress of wounds, fitted and applied casts, and prepped men for surgery. This tireless crew made weekly rounds of the wards, but it was here in the cast room where the real toil was done.

The wounded, arriving daily from Vietnam, were straining the hospital's facilities. Men on litter beds waited on each side of me. Less critically wounded men, along with other casualties from accidents or illness, filled the hallway in a long line.

There was little talk as we waited. Each of us was living in our own little world of pain, fear, and uncertainty.

The corpsman wheeled me to a young doctor who quickly scratched his signature on a form the man held out to him. Then the doctor picked up my medical record and started reading it. "Man," he said, studying the form, "they really got you, didn't they?" Then he summarized aloud the main points on my chart: "Traumatic amputation of right arm below elbow with multiple contusions, residual shrapnel and drainage. Surgical amputation of left leg above the knee. Amputation of right leg above the knee. Tracheotomy. Superficial shrapnel in lung, stomach and groin area. Shrapnel and scar tissue on left side of neck."

"I don't look too good on paper, do I, Doc?"

"Let's take a look at those stumps," he said briskly.

The attendant drew back the sheet, and I tensed myself for the coming ordeal.

"Will you give me some Demerol?" I pleaded.

"You've had your last shot of Demerol for a while," he stated. "You don't want us to turn you into a junkie on top of everything else, do you?"

As his examination progressed, the pain grew intense. I found myself not caring whether I would become a junkie or not.

He completed his inspection, and while the corpsman rebandaged my wounds, the young doctor perched on a stool beside my litter bed and started to talk.

"Your right leg is coming along fine. It's healing well. But your left leg and right arm will probably need a skin graft. For now, I want you to try to get your strength back. We'll exercise you in bed, even while the stumps are healing. We'll have to clean your wounds each week and change your dressings until we get you to the point where we can do the skin graft. After that, we'll send you to physical therapy. We'll see how your stumps heal before we decide what to do about fitting you with limbs."

I came alive at the word "limbs." "What about artificial limbs?" I asked. "Will I be able to walk? I mean, will I be able to walk out of this place?"

He studied my chart, tapped his pencil on it reflectively, then looked up at me with compassion in his eyes. "I can't say now. No one can say." He put his hand on my arm. "Look," he said quietly, "you have no knees. In order to walk you'll need crutches to compensate for the lack of balance your knees would have given you. But with only one arm, we don't know whether you can handle crutches."

His voice softened. "There's another factor. The body can only stand so much. We can only hang so many artificial limbs on you. There's the question of tolerance, of irritation, and of physical endurance." He began collecting his papers. "Beyond a certain point," he added resignedly, "it just isn't worth it."

I raised on my left elbow. "I'm willing to try anything," I pleaded. "I'll put out as much effort as is necessary."

He rose to go. "I know, I know," he answered. "But even on artificial limbs you won't be all that independent." He stood at my side, looking at the empty place under the sheet.

"What if you fall down?"

For a moment I was a bit shaken at his question.

"Well, I'll get up."

He shook his head. "You won't be able to. Without knees, you can't get up."

I stared back at him stunned. He dropped his eyes and left the room.

As an aide wheeled me back down hallways, the drab-green ceiling seemed like an endless curtain falling down on me.

Ever since the injury, I had believed that anybody could use artificial limbs, that there would always be some way to walk again. I knew that it would take hard work and time. But it had not occurred to me that if I fell down I would be unable to get back up again.

I was wheeled into an elevator and the door closed with a bang. Panic hit me. With all its technological splendor, I had been convinced that the United States could devise ways for a triple-amputee to get around under his own power.

Now, it seemed otherwise. I would not reenter society as I had left it. From now on I would always be different and set apart from others. How exactly, I didn't yet know.

The elevator shuddered to a stop at my floor. The wheels of my litter bed clattered over the floor sill, and I was moved swiftly down a long corridor. I could hear the rapid footsteps of the man pushing it and his breathing as he exerted the muscles in his healthy limbs.

He, like most others in the world, had two arms and two legs. I wondered if he realized how lucky he was. Slowly a tear slid down the side of my face and onto the pillow.

7

LAUGH OR CRY

"To live is to suffer. To survive is to find meaning in suffering."

— Dr. Viktor Frankl

"They tell me you were with the Cav!" rasped a voice on my right.

With tears so close to the surface, I was in no mood to talk. "What's it to you?" I finally croaked, keeping my eyes on the ceiling.

"To hell with you then!" snapped the voice.

I didn't look at my neighbor but could hear him grunt and turn over in bed. Soon he was snoring.

I tried to sleep too, but it was impossible. So I began to look around my new home which they called the Snake Pit. It was empty now except for the two of us. I turned my head to look at him. He had on civilian pajamas. I thought that curious. Resting on top of his bed covers beside him was his arm cast. That was odd. He apparently took it off whenever he felt like it. At first, I was surprised by such irreverence. But he had his fingers—all of them. And his legs too.

The seriousness of my situation sank deeper into me. To fight back the anguish, I continued my examination. Our ward was at the end of a wing of the officer orthopedic area called Ward One. Our small enclave—the Snake Pit—contained eight standard hospital beds spaced evenly in a U-shaped pattern. Each bed unit had a side table, a nurses' call button, a metal locker, and a small, black-and-white TV set. Bright sunlight flooded the room from large windows on three sides.

On the middle of the tiled floor, someone had painted a large, writhing, stylized, gold snake, now worn by wear.

The gentle snoring from the next bed had such a lulling quality to it that I became drowsy and fell asleep.

"If you ain't Airborne, you ain't worth a damn!" It was the same loud, raspy voice on my right. My eyes slowly focused on the ceiling tiles as I awakened.

"Will you knock it off?" I muttered angrily.

"Hey, he's alive after all," crowed the voice.

I turned my head toward the tormentor. Bright, darting eyes gleamed at me from a lean face under a thinning, black hairline. He appeared to be in his late 20s.

"Who are you?" I retorted.

"They call me Jack—Nasty Jack."

Soon I knew why. Every sentence he uttered was punctuated with profanity.

"What did he say?" Nasty Jack asked.

"What did *who* say?" I countered.

"Don't play games with me. What did *he* say?"

"You mean the doctor up in the cast room?"

"Right."

"He said it would take some time and uh . . . uh . . . that I shouldn't expect to move about much."

"Listen." He was sitting on the edge of his bed now, looking at me intently. "Whatever he said, forget it."

There was more profanity, and he stood up and approached my bed.

"Anybody says you won't walk out of this outfit—the hell with 'em!" He began pacing back and forth between our beds. "What do these idiots here know about fighting—or living—or dying? Nothing! I know—and you know."

He stopped in front of me and leaned into my face. I stared back at him. "So you're going to make it. If you ever forget it, I will personally kick your butt."

He turned to walk away but suddenly stopped and wheeled about. "Besides," he grinned, "you're Airborne, aren't you?"

In those early days in the Snake Pit, my emotions were on a roller-coaster. Within the same minute I could be exhilarated and depressed. Laughter and tears often welled up in me during the same sentence.

The high spirits and constant banter in our ward were, of course, a desperate attempt by everyone to keep from sliding into a deep depression. The tumultuous emotions of most of the men in the "pit" made it dangerous territory for young nurses. But there was one nurse we couldn't intimidate. Major Baker.

"She could've been a lieutenant colonel by now, or even higher," commented Nasty Jack one morning as he watched her storm out of the room after scolding him for not wearing his cast.

He leaned over to me. "She's one of those rare people—one who truly loves her work. She's turned down a lot of administrative jobs and staff duty, and it's cost her more than one promotion. After 30 years in the Army nurse corps she's still only a major? The way she takes care of us, she ought to be a general!"

There was a clamor of footsteps in the hall. Nasty Jack groaned, "Here she comes now on another one of those clean-up rampages."

The major marched back in, trailed by a crew of corpsmen she had pulled off of other assignments. Barking orders like a battlefield commander, she stood in the middle of the ward while the corpsmen, armed with brooms, mops, and buckets, tore into the floors, walls, and even the ceiling. After a time of intense disruption, the corpsmen gathered up their equipment and departed. Major Baker gave us a benign smile, as if she knew a secret, turned on her heels and disappeared.

In the days that followed, I learned a lot about Captain "Nasty Jack" Lawton. During his second tour in Vietnam as a company commander with the 101st Airborne, he and his men were on a sweep west of Tam Ky when the North Vietnamese opened up on them with rockets, mortars, and automatic weapons. Jack took 22 rounds in his arm, leg, and shoulder from a Chinese automatic rifle. He kept on fighting and actually rescued some of the other wounded.

After being evacuated to a rear area, Jack was met by an NBC-TV news team headed by the late Frank McGee. Right there they filmed Jack's version of the action. McGee later told Jack that it was the best combat interview he had ever obtained—but he couldn't use it because of Lawton's steady stream of profanity. When the guys in the "pit" learned about the incident, Lawton was forever branded as Nasty Jack.

Jack loved his profane and irreverent role in the "pit." While out on pass one night, Jack ended up in a strippers' bar on 14th Street. Approaching the star dancer he said, "Honey, I got some friends back at Walter Reed Hospital who sure would like to see a beautiful woman like you."

Jack could charm the scales off a snake. In no time, he had a coat around the scantily clad stripper. They caught a cab back to Walter Reed where he sneaked her past the nurses' station and into the "pit."

The lights were dim and the men asleep. "Now, Honey,"

whispered Jack, "go around to each bed and kiss every one of those guys and let them know what they were fighting for!" She did and ended her rounds with a helicopter pilot, a fresh casualty on heavy medication who had just come in earlier in the evening. At the girl's kiss, he awoke in a dazed stupor, gazed at her blankly for a moment and fell back unconscious.

Jack wanted to stir up a little more fun. "Honey, would you dance for us a little bit?"

"I cain't dance without no music," said the girl with a shake of her blonde tresses. By this time, everyone but the helicopter pilot was wide awake. Someone found a small phonograph, but the only record available was "The Star Spangled Banner."

The stripper climbed onto the table, threw her coat to Nasty Jack, and started bumping and grinding to the national anthem—and the wild applause of her audience.

Next morning, the helicopter pilot awoke and told the man next to him, "This medication must be getting to me. I had the strangest dream last night. I dreamt that this girl came up and kissed me here in bed. And she was almost stark naked!"

Self-pity perched on our bedsteads like a gargoyle, waiting to leap on us at any opportunity. Late one afternoon a nurse had wheeled me to the roof of the hospital entrance portico. I sat by myself bathed in a weak May sun staring over the parapet at the grounds. It was my first real look at America in a year. I spotted the cars in the parking lot and suddenly realized I had never seen some of the models before and didn't know their names.

Then I noticed a soldier walking up the long, curved walk toward our building, heading under the portico beneath me. My gaze zoomed in on a familiar yellow patch on his shoulder. Right in the center of it was the black horsehead!

"Hey, Sarge," I called down excitedly. "First Cav, all the w-a-a-y!"

He didn't look up. Apparently he never heard me. He just kept walking and disappeared below. I sank back into a sickening sadness. I knew I would never be part of the Cav again, never be part of the Army again, and worst of all, never be what I once was again.

But the other guys in the "pit" helped me fight self-pity by teaching me to laugh rather than cry. For example, there was Weird Harold. Like Nasty Jack, he was another character in the "pit" who helped break reality down into manageable portions. He had taken a lot of shrapnel and lost a leg and an eye. Plastic surgeons hadn't as yet worked on his face, and it was a mess. He looked weird and everybody called him just that.

Inevitably, there would be a visit to the ward by one of the elderly "Gray Ladies" who pushed an orange-juice cart as her chore to care for the nation's wounded. Naturally, she would come across Weird Harold.

The reaction was always the same.

"Well, young man, what happened to you?"

Weird Harold went into his act.

"Well, ma'am," he would deadpan, "I know it sounds a bit strange, but I came in here one day for a dental checkup and got run over by a food cart."

We loved it.

Our newspapers and bedside television sets told us about the many thousands of Americans in cities around the country marching against the war. Just watching this on the evening news could be a downer. One night the commentator on my set was giving us the latest from Vietnam. More bad news.

"Cut that stuff off!" yelled Nasty Jack. "It's time for 'Laugh In.'"

I quickly switched on Channel 4, and soon my leg and arm stumps were throbbing as I laughed at the antics of Dan Rowan and Dick Martin. Saturday morning cartoons were also on our list of TV favorites. For all of us, humor was the great tension reliever.

Visitors played a crucial role. DeWitt and Winnette Buice, Lithonian neighbors during my boyhood, were now living in Arlington, Virginia. They were the first to stop in. Then Mom and Dad flew up from Georgia the very first weekend after my arrival at Walter Reed.

I dreaded their visit. How would they react when they saw they had only half a son left?

To ensure privacy, I requested a visiting room for our reunion. From its window, I could look out onto the building's front sidewalk and watch their arrival.

My throat tensed when I saw them coming up the walk, my dad in that familiar rolling gait, Mother anxiously looking up at the windows. What could I do to break the tension?

When they began climbing the entrance steps, I yelled out the hospital window: "Well, look what's coming—another march on Washington!"

They stopped short, then burst into nervous laughter.

The ice was broken.

My parents walked hesitantly into the room where I sat in a wheelchair. Much about them had changed and much hadn't. Dad looked a little older but still managed a broad grin. My mother required a little more makeup around her eyes, but I caught the familiar aroma of her perfume.

We all embraced. It was painful to see them holding reins on their emotions when they looked at my body. I knew they wanted to cry and didn't dare.

Dad spoke first. "You're looking good, son." He said it over and over throughout their visit.

Mother took a different approach. "Max, you're too *thin*." When a ward doctor came in, she followed him back into the hall where I knew she was asking all kinds of questions. What

he said gave her little satisfaction. I could see her standing outside the door, tears streaming down her face.

In less than half an hour, my strength drained away. My parents reluctantly said good-bye, promising to return the next day,
which was Sunday.

"We'll take you out for a good meal, Max," said Mom, kiss-
ing me. It would be my first trip outside the hospital.

The next day, my parents came with the Buices. With the
help of an aide, they wheeled me to the Buices' car which was
parked at the curb. Then the three men stood looking at me.

I tried to joke with them. "What's the matter. Don't any of
you know which end to grab?"

The aide suggested they lift me under my armpits. With
much grunting and straining, they lifted me from the wheelchair to the front seat of the car. The car started. Although we
were going quite slowly, it seemed fast to me, as it had been a
long time since I had ridden in a car. When Mr. Buice stepped
on the brake, instinctively I moved to brace my feet against the
floorboard. Instead, I bolted forward and almost hit the dash-
board. Quickly I buckled my seat belt.

The late spring countryside in Maryland was beautiful.
Dogwood bloomed along the road, and the rolling fields were a
brilliant green. The air seemed so fresh after the staleness of the
hospital. We pulled up to a country restaurant, and Dad and
Mr. Buice were able to work my wheelchair into the lounge
where we waited for a table.

The room was crowded with laughing, talking men and
women, many standing at the bar sipping drinks before dinner.
When I noticed some of them staring at me, I felt uneasy.

"Can you wheel me outside?" I asked the two men. There
we waited quietly in the warm spring sun until our table was
ready.

I don't remember what I had for dinner that day. All I recall is that as we sat at a white linen-covered table, I realized that the awkward, self-conscious stares of people would go with me for the rest of my life.

8

THERAPY

"That which does not kill me makes me stronger."

— FRIEDRICH NIETZSCHE

"What 'cha been doin' all morning?" someone asked Nasty Jack as he strolled confidently into the "pit," carrying something in his limp hand.

"I've just made the cutest little wooden box you ever did see," he chortled.

He turned to me. "Don't laugh, Cleland. They'll soon have you making these sweet little things in therapy, too."

As I grew a bit stronger, "therapy" became the watchword of my life at Walter Reed. A physical therapist started visiting me the first week. My wounds had not yet healed, and my arm stump still drained.

"You've got to exercise the muscles in your legs and arms," he said.

"How do I do that?"

He explained that I'd have to learn to exercise in bed, using what was left of my muscles. Specifically, he wanted me to exercise my two "legs" and my almost nonexistent arm by pushing against his hand which he held up as resistance for my muscles.

"I don't think I can do it."

"You *can* do it," he insisted.

Straining, I pushed weakly, limb by limb, until I had nothing left.

The therapist was quiet for a moment. "Captain Cleland, you use it or lose it."

"What do you mean?"

"I mean that if you don't use your right arm stump, your shoulder will become frozen in place. And if you don't exercise your leg stumps, the muscles in your thighs will shrink."

Gritting my teeth, I pushed against his hand again and again. As I continued this exercise day after day, I realized that, amazingly enough, I was getting strong at these broken places. The muscles that were left began developing and compensating for muscles that had been lost. Slowly, ever so slowly, my body was beginning to adjust to its new shape and the new demands placed on it. Hope began to grow in me again.

One of my early struggles was learning how to dress myself.

It was difficult. Shirts especially took time to master. I learned to button my left shirt sleeve first before slipping my arm into it. Then I rolled up the sleeve on the right side. The trousers presented a different problem. First I inserted my left stump, pulling up the pants and tucking in the shirt as I went. Then I did the same on the right side. After stretching out on my back, I pulled up the pants all the way with a rocking motion. Fastening a belt wasn't too difficult, but pulling up a zipper with one hand was a battle. I learned not to untie my ties, but to just loosen them into large circles and pull them on and off over my head.

As I got better able to do things for myself, even my social life began to improve. I remembered Joy, a girl I had dated when I lived in Washington. She had later married a close friend of mine. But after a short time, he died, so she was single again. I called her up on the ward phone from my bed.

"Max!" she squealed. "You're back from Vietnam! How are you?"

"Well, Joy, I kinda got hurt over there a little bit."

The phone was quiet.

"Uh . . . uh," I strained, "more than a little hurt, I guess. I got pretty badly banged up."

I told her the story.

"We've both been hurt," she said quietly.

I asked her if she would come and see me.

"Sure," she exclaimed. "Will they let me on the ward?"

I sat propped in a wheelchair, wearing fresh pajamas and a robe when Joy arrived. When she first saw me, for just an instant, something like a quick cloud-shadow crossing a summer meadow touched her face. Then her smile became radiant.

"Max!" she cried, running over to me. As she leaned down and embraced me, I drank deep of her soft, feminine warmth, her perfumed aroma. She pushed my wheelchair to the private visitor's room, and we talked a long time about the old days.

She returned a few days later and took me out in her car to a drive-in hamburger place. As we drove down 16th Street, a passing truck backfired, and I ducked down into the seat.

"Max, are you all right?" she exclaimed.

"Yes," I said sheepishly. "Better be careful never to pop your chewing gum."

Joy returned several times for visits, again taking me out to drive-ins where we consumed hamburgers and milkshakes like two high-school kids on a date. Though our relationship remained on a friendship basis, Joy helped to restore my feelings of masculinity. It was possible for a girl to relate to me as a human being.

As my outlook brightened, I became more open with other patients. I met a fellow from the ward across the hall who had also been with the First Air Cavalry Division at Khe Sanh. He had been in a rocket attack and a piece of shrapnel had cut his larynx out. He could talk only by gulping air and forcing it back up through his esophagus.

"I sound like Popeye," he grinned. He explained that the doctors were going to do an operation in which they would attempt to make a kind of larynx in connection with his esophagus. "You know," he gulped enthusiastically, "I feel like I've got a second life to live!"

I nodded, thinking to myself that he certainly did. *After all, you've got all your limbs. I should be so lucky.*

One day, Major Baker brought me a new wheelchair.

"It's a one-hand drive," she explained, showing me the double-ring handgrip on the left wheel. "The smaller ring is for the right wheel, and the larger one is for the left wheel." Soon I was careening around hospital corridors with great zest. After crashing into a few water coolers and startling some nurses, I learned how to handle it. I was mobile!

By this time I was strong enough to go to physical therapy clinic. There I did leg pushups on a gym mat. A rolled towel was inserted underneath what remained of each leg, and I pushed off the towel, raising my back off the mat. Switching from one leg to the other, I eventually worked up to 100 pushups per leg.

I met another triple-amputee there. He had lost both arms and a leg in Vietnam. As we talked, there was something familiar about him; his eyes were large and round. Then I remembered. He was the guy next to me in the ambulance going to the airport in Japan. I recalled him desperately sucking a Coke through a straw. I had felt certain he wouldn't make it.

As we did our exercises, he looked at me and grinned. "Good seeing you do those, Max. You know, when I saw you in that ambulance in Japan, I thought you were a goner for sure."

After therapy one day, Nasty Jack stuck his head inside the "pit" and casually informed me, "They're having a party tonight. You ought to get off your tail and go with us."

It was my first invitation from the gang in the "pit" to go "outside." Yet I was a little hesitant and queried Jack about the party.

"It's an open house in some nurse's apartment," he said. "Several of them live together in Maryland. They've invited a lot of doctors and some other guys on the ward. Get your stuff together, and we'll pick you up about eight."

Jack didn't even give me a chance to turn him down. Before I could think about it, three guys grabbed me and wheeled me off the ward and outside. Then they dumped me into the front seat of a small Chevrolet, gave me a borrowed sports coat and hauled me out to Silver Spring for my first social event as a triple-amputee.

"Be careful with these young nurses," Jack joked as he beat on the door with his cast.

I didn't sip much punch that night because I found that when the alcohol hit my heart and started it pumping, the ends of my legs and arm—which had not quite healed yet—throbbed painfully.

As I sat there in my wheelchair amid the hubbub of party conversation and laughter, I felt like a wallflower. But I knew that if I didn't make at least a small effort to meet people, I might shy away from parties forever. So, with just enough punch in me to help me struggle out of my shell, I sallied forth. It was awkward going up to people, not having learned how to shake hands and hold my punch glass at the same time. I could try to look debonair by holding firmly onto the glass with my left hand, or I could set it on the floor and shake hands. I tried the latter—only to lose my drink under someone's foot. So I ended up parking my glass by the punch bowl, circling the room to meet people and then returning to my glass.

To my astonishment, I became part of the crowd that evening. Late that night, after getting back to the ward, I lay in my bed thinking about it. Most everybody at that party had all their arms and legs. But they all had worries or problems. Some had shared their concerns with me, thinking that I could understand their personal hurt since I had been hurt myself. This was a surprise to me. I didn't think I had anything to offer. But apparently I did. It taught me a lesson: most people are so caught up in their own troubles they rarely have time to be aware of yours. After that party, I realized I could be of help to people who had been broken in different ways.

I was still thinking about my first night out when one of the men in our ward came in with a long face. "Did 'ja hear about the guy across the hall?"

"What guy?"

"The one with the Popeye voice who had his esophagus operation yesterday."

"What about him?" I asked.

"He seemed all right when they wheeled him back to his room. Then he hemorrhaged." My fellow patient lowered his head. "He couldn't cry out, and the nurses' call button didn't work. And he died."

I turned my head away. This was the grateful guy who had felt like he had been given a second chance at life.

Staring at the dark window, I thought, *How very fragile life is. You can be saved on the battlefield and die in some dumb accident.*

It was a sharp reminder to me that life should never be taken for granted.

9

OUTSIDE

"Change is good. You go first."

— SEEN IN A *DILBERT* CARTOON

Each morning, I couldn't take my eyes off one of the patients in our ward, Carl Nunziato, as he put on his legs. He had been fitted with two gleaming, plastic, flesh-colored limbs which he parked beside his bed like a bicycle.

One morning, I watched his slow progress as he put them on before leaving for therapy. It took him almost half an hour. Straining and wincing, he drew on heavy woolen socks over his leg stumps, then inserted them into the rigid set of laminated plastic casts. After that, he anchored the plastic limbs to his thighs with heavy leather straps. Lifting himself erect on two crutches, he leaned forward on them and began shifting his body to swing each leg ahead of the other. By the time he had walked across the room, sweat was running down his pain-lined face. Then he collapsed in a chair.

"Com' on, baby, get up and use 'em," someone yelled. The other guys in the "pit" knew about the "use-it-or-lose-it" philosophy of PT, and they gave Carl little sympathy. If it was tough for him, I knew it would be worse for me. Carl had both knees, and I had none.

One day, when the "pit" was empty except for the two of us, Carl and I had a chance to talk. I trusted Carl because, except for me, he was the most disabled guy on the ward. I asked him to level with me about the difference between being in the hospital and being out in the world.

"You'll get along fine in the hospital," he said. "They've got things to take care of you here—ramps for your wheelchair, wide enough johns. You get your chow fixed, your bed made. Here there are people who understand you, who care about you. You can go out on dates with girls in groups with the other guys here and not feel out of place."

He glanced out the window, and I saw his expression change. "When you go outside on your own, then it'll get tough."

I looked out the window toward the tree-filled skyline, the distant buildings, streets, and stores. The outside. According to Carl, it was the enemy. It might be the enemy, but I knew I had to face it sooner or later.

In mid-June, about two months after returning to the States, I dared to take my first weekend pass.

It was a carefully planned weekend. I had phoned Darlene, a girl I had dated before I went to Vietnam. We had continued writing, and Darlene, who lived in a northeastern state, knew of my injuries. I couldn't think of anyone with whom I'd rather share this pass.

"Yes, Max," she had agreed with enthusiasm on the phone, "I'd love to join you in Washington!" I asked her to fly down, then planned an itinerary of fun. Since I spent very little money overseas I had a lot saved up. I reserved the largest suite in the Washington Hilton with a room for her and one for me. The guys in the "pit" seemed as excited about it as I was. Outside of a few short trips with Joy, this would be my first real date.

Friday afternoon—to the accompaniment of whoops and shouts of encouragement—I proudly wheeled out of the ward. "See ya Sunday, fellas!" I called. A cab dropped me off in front of the Washington Hilton, where flags fluttered in a June breeze. I paid the driver and wheeled into the hotel lobby where I checked my reservation.

Then, with pounding heart, I parked my chair on the side of the lobby and pretended to read a magazine while keeping an eye peeled on the entrance.

There she was, right on time!

I wheeled up and greeted her. Talking excitedly together, we headed for the suite, trailed by a bellhop carrying her suitcase. Finally, in the room, I tipped the bellboy. Then Darlene and I settled down on an overstuffed sofa and began to talk.

About 20 minutes went by as we caught up on each other's life. But the conversation grew strained. Darlene kept her eyes averted from me and seemed nervous.

I started to tell her about the various shows we were going to see when she looked at her watch. "Oh my," she exclaimed. "My plane is leaving at 4:30 this afternoon. I must be going."

I sat rooted in shock, voiceless. She stood up and walked over to her suitcase.

"Uh . . . uh," I stammered foolishly, "can I help you?"

"Oh please, no. I can handle it," she said, quickly starting for the door. "Well," she said brightly, turning her face to me with a forced smile, "it has been good seeing you, Max. Good-bye." And she walked out.

I sat staring at the door for a long time. Finally, I wheeled my chair into the hall and took the elevator down to the hotel bar where I ordered a whiskey sour.

After five of them, I propelled myself into the restaurant where I had dinner and made passes at each waitress who came by. By midnight, I was trying to date the cashier. They all smiled or laughed, which made me feel even more embarrassed.

Finally, at 12:30 A.M., my stumps aching from the alcohol, I made my way upstairs to the cavernous, empty suite and tumbled into bed muttering, "The hell with it."

Early the next morning, as I rolled slowly back into the Snake Pit, there was a welcome silence. Mercifully, no one said anything.

One of the toughest adjustments was made by "No Way" Dave Alligood. Dave, a small, stocky, dark-haired man, had been shot up badly in Vietnam. One of his legs was shattered to the point where Walter Reed doctors were ready to take it off. Dave kept insisting that it be given a chance to heal.

Reluctantly they agreed but told him he would have to undergo a complex skin graft operation. They would have to grow skin from his stomach to one of his arms, then transfer it to his wounded leg. It would be a long and painstaking ordeal that would take months. Dave agreed.

In the meantime, he had fallen in love with one of the physical therapists, and they had set a wedding date which fell between the stomach graft and the leg graft. Right after they were married, Dave was wrapped like a pretzel in a body cast. He had to move about while doubled over, with one arm carrying the skin pouch attached to the calf of his leg. He was frozen in this bent-over position for months. Occasionally, we would taunt the new bridegroom by whispering across the beds: "No way! No way!"

Dave and his bride beat the odds. She got pregnant.

We never figured out how they did it.

Anything could be done, I decided, if a person put his mind to it.

Now that I was in an expanded therapy program, I had an adjustment to make, too. A skin graft operation on my arm was a success, and I had been fitted with an artificial arm which had a hook on the end.

"But what about one of those nice-looking plastic hands?" I asked.

"That will come later," said the therapist. "Believe me, Max, you'll find the hook more useful."

The artificial arm slipped onto a small piece of bone and muscle that remained below my right elbow. A shoulder strap anchored to my upper left arm fitted across my back. From it, a cable went to the hand hook, which was held tightly closed by rubber bands. By flexing and relaxing my shoulders, the cable would open and close the hook. I was quite proud of my new hand and figured this limb-fitting business wasn't going to be so bad after all.

With the advent of the arm, my rehab program now expanded to include occupational therapy. It had little to do with occupations of any kind, but it was therapy. I wasn't particularly interested, though, because moving checkers about a board and picking up papers with my hook became boring. What really intrigued me at these sessions was the possibility of driving a car. Excitement rose within me every time I thought of it. Could a car be hooked up for a person like me? The therapist showed me a steering wheel with a ring attached which could be grasped with a hook. But the gadget looked almost impossible to manage. For a while, driving a car would not be for me.

My therapist continued to spark my spirits, however. She was an attractive, young brunette, right out of occupational therapy school at Brooke Army Hospital in Texas.

I was her first patient.

When she saw me she cried.

As we got to know each other, I looked forward to my sessions with her because after the work we could go off in a corner, have a cup of coffee and talk. I once showed her a snapshot of how I used to look in uniform before I was injured.

She gazed at it a long time, then looked up at me with moist eyes. "I'll always think of you this way, Max."

Brightening up, she said, "We've got to do a bilateral project, you know."

That intrigued me. As a college history major, I had learned that a "bilateral" project meant two countries working together on a special job. This would bring the two of us even closer together.

I was wrong. "Bilateral," in the therapeutic sense, meant making something with my two "hands." I was crushed. Once again my spirits fell. "Well," I said in resignation, "I'm not going to make any of those blasted little wooden boxes."

I didn't.

I made a wooden doorstop.

While napping one Saturday afternoon, I was awakened by a shrill voice shouting, "Well, boys, here it is!" I looked up through sleep-blurred eyes to see a heavyset woman in a flamboyant, flowered hat and a loud orange and green dress swinging a gallon of bourbon.

It was Wilma. Someone called her Baltimore's one-woman Chamber of Commerce. She was here to produce what soon became a tradition in the ward: the "pit party." On this day Wilma brought enough refreshments to cheer up all the guys. Later, as the "pit" parties became perfected, she would bring Playboy bunnies and other girlfriends down from Baltimore.

Wilma had a flair for promotion. She once corralled a Baltimore brewing company into furnishing a truckload of beer and three bands for the guys on the wards. One Saturday afternoon, she filled two Army buses with patients from the hospital and took us to Baltimore. Our eyes bugged out when we pulled up in front of stripper Blaze Starr's Two O'Clock Club. Somehow we all managed to squeeze into the place.

Built like a redheaded Greek goddess, Blaze welcomed us in her West Virginia drawl. She had men in her own family who had fought in Vietnam, she said. Blaze knew that we patients in Walter Reed liked to be reminded that we were men, and she did this in the nicest, most compassionate way.

Once she came to the hospital as part of a variety show held in the Walter Reed Red Cross hall. Many big-name acts were present including Flip Wilson and some top singing groups. Blaze arrived in a beautiful dress and spent her time circulating among us. When one of the groups on stage began playing a catchy number, some of the men got up and started dancing in the aisle. I noticed a young black man in his early 20s sitting quietly in a corner of the hall, dressed in his robe and pajamas. He had been blinded in Vietnam by shrapnel. Blaze saw him and asked if he'd like to dance. He nodded, rose, and together the two of them danced slowly. The look on that young man's face was pure joy.

An old girlfriend was coming to see me! When she peeked around the corner of our ward entrance, I was elated.

"Let me show you some Washington sights, and then I'll buy you lunch!" I offered. As her face lit up, I glowed with pride.

We took a cab to Lafayette Park across from the White House. It was one of those bright, brisk days so unusual during

Washington's muggy summers. The sidewalks were alive with cheerful-looking people. A fresh breeze brought a sharp scent of new-mown grass mingled with traffic fumes from busy Pennsylvania Avenue. As we viewed the picturesque panorama of the White House from the park, we reminisced about old times.

When we continued our sidewalk tour, I could sense her delicate, young body pushing my chair. Normally, I would have been propelling myself, but we had a few blocks to travel.

"It's so good to be with you again, Max," she said happily.

"What there is of me," I tried to laugh.

"No," she chided, "you're all there—the Max I knew," she added softly.

I reached over my shoulder and squeezed her slender hand.

As we approached the crossing, the front wheels of my chair dropped off the curb. Suddenly I pitched forward into the gutter of Pennsylvania Avenue, directly across from the White House. For several moments I lay in the dirt and cigarette butts, frantically scrambling about, one-armed and legless, like a fish flopping on a riverbank.

I looked up into horrified faces of onlookers frozen in shock. Agonizing embarrassment flooded me as I clumsily tried to wrest my torso upright. I couldn't bear to look at the girl with whom I had been talking so confidently.

Then I was staring into an oncoming, blinking yellow light—the directional signal of a car turning toward me. I cried out. Two men rushed from the watching crowd, lifted me to the sidewalk and back into the wheelchair. I sank in the sling-seat gasping, trying to thank them.

My companion was almost hysterical, crying over and over. "I'm sorry, Max! I'm sorry!"

I tried to comfort her. "Don't worry, honey," I soothed, "it was my fault. I'll have to remember that wheelchairs go off curbs backwards."

She attempted to brush the dirt off my empty trouser legs and I stopped her. "That's all right," I muttered quickly tucking them under my stumps.

She dried her tears with a handkerchief, and the crowd of curious onlookers broke up and drifted away. I looked up and forced a grin. "Let's go have lunch."

We hailed a cab which took us to the Rive Gauche Restaurant in Georgetown for lunch—but I couldn't enjoy it. The hot shame of the spill still seared me like a burn that continued to throb. I tried to forget it and thought about the day I first met her. I was 24 then, and stood six feet, two inches.

Now I was in a wheelchair. Is this all that was left for me? To be hauled around like a sack of grain for the rest of my life?

10

HOMETOWN WELCOME

"You can't go home again."

— THOMAS WOLFE

An explosion of applause split the hot, muggy air as they carried me off the commercial jet in Atlanta. I gave a thumbs-up sign to the cheering crowd of welcomers—but wore sunglasses so they wouldn't see the fear in my eyes. I felt terribly embarrassed to be returning home in a wheelchair.

As we moved on out of the airport, reporters kept pace with my wheelchair, asking questions, holding microphones for my comments. I was rushed to a waiting car, and Mom and Dad were ushered in with me.

"Max," said Mom adoringly, "it's a motorcade. They're going to escort us all the way home."

Two policemen ahead of us mounted motorcycles and stamped on the starters. They settled down on their cycle seats and looked back. The official in our car motioned them on, engines roared, our motorcade started up, and we swung out of the airport.

As we moved along, with sirens piercing the steamy July air and the sun shimmering on the highway, I recognized the scenery. There were the same pine trees, the same gray granite outcroppings. Then the sign: Lithonia City Limits. As we came to my street, I saw suspended across the road a giant, fluttering banner: WELCOME HOME MAX!

Tears filled my eyes. As we approached the house, I saw that our street and front lawn were crowded with people. There stood my old high school band. The leader was watching over his shoulder. When he saw us turn the corner he brought his arms down in a flourish and the band struck up the "Star Spangled Banner."

Many hands reached to help me out of the car. I felt so vulnerable seeing my old friends and having to greet them with one hand. I noticed a lady who had once taught in the elementary school standing off to one side by a tree. I knew she had a son in Vietnam. She had pulled a leafy bough down to hide the tears streaming down her face.

And there was Elmer. He and I had worked in the same general store in Lithonia where I had been employed after school hours. Elmer was black and had a son in Vietnam. Then he told me that his son had been blown up outside of Saigon and had lost both his arms and legs.

As tears streamed down his craggy face, I held his work-hardened hand and assured him that I knew his son was going to be all right.

Finally, the crowd began to thin, and I was helped into the house. Dad had constructed a long, sloping ramp to ease my way in.

I wheeled into my old room. It had been kept just as I had left it—the medals, the trophies, even the silver *Atlanta Journal* cup, now slightly tarnished after almost a decade. Nothing had changed—except me.

I had been given a hero's welcome, but I did not feel like a hero. I thought of what had happened since I had left this room. I had seen young men die. I had lost my courage. I had almost been killed.

I wheeled into the quiet living room. Mom hovered at my side, her dark eyes concerned behind her glasses. "Do you need a cushion?" "Are you comfortable in that chair?" "Can I get you . . . ?"

"No, Mom," I interrupted, waving her away, "I'm okay, just fine." I wheeled over to the stereo set that had been shipped from Japan, feeling grateful to the sergeant who had done this for me.

Then I saw the stuff on the wall. My parents had hung certificates for the Soldier's Medal which I had been awarded for allegedly shielding my men from the grenade blast and the Silver Star for allegedly coming to the aid of wounded troops in the night of the Khe Sanh rocket attack.

I winced. There were no heroics on which to base the Soldier's Medal. And it had been my men who took care of the wounded during the rocket attack, not me. Some compassionate military men had obviously recommended me for the Silver Star, but I didn't deserve it.

"Mom."

She hurried into the room. "Yes?"

"There is one thing you can do for me. Please take down those awards."

I had worn my uniform home, but it was hot and I wanted to get out of it and into some fun clothes. I wanted desperately to get back into my old lifestyle again. I remembered a popular Peachtree Street nightclub in downtown Atlanta—a great dancing spot. With some friends, I went to the city that night and headed for the old bar.

We were laughing and bantering as we moved down the sidewalk when I found myself staring at a longhaired youth sauntering in front of us. A U.S. flag was sewn on the rear of his tattered jeans, and he was wearing an oversized Army fatigue jacket. It was the same kind of jacket medics had cut off of me just months earlier.

My gut twisted, and I stopped talking.

"That jacket . . ." I muttered.

"Hey Max." It was one of my friends leaning down. "Relax," he said calmly, "the war's over for you."

The nightclub looked pretty much the same, but I wasn't prepared for the sounds. Instead of the light rock music I had been accustomed to before leaving for Vietnam, I was hit by explosive, psychedelic, hard rock numbers popularized by groups I had never even heard of.

"Ladeez an' genamun." The band leader who stood in front of us was known to booze it up a little too much, and he was certainly now well into the sauce. "We have with us here in the club tonight, Max Cleland, Atlanta's favorite son, who has just come home from Vietnam—winner of the Purple Heart. Let's show him we appreciate him. Let's hear it for Max!"

He had the spotlight on me while the band gave a fanfare. The crowd applauded loudly. I gave a weak wave—and felt even weaker inside because I was not entitled to the Purple Heart either, since I was not wounded by enemy action.

Someone shoved a drink at me. The waitress nodded at another table. "It's the compliments of . . ." More drinks came, and soon I was back into the spirit of things.

Almost.

Watching the couples on the dance floor, my stomach began to sink more and more. I began to really feel sorry for myself. The more drinks I had, the more my melancholy deepened.

I went back to the club several times while I was home.

Each time it was worse. The cycle was always the same—self-pity, booze, depression. I felt more and more ridiculous in the wheelchair at a dancing spot, especially since the band leader kept escalating my supposed heroism. The last time I visited the club he introduced me as a "winna of the Medal of Honna."

I left the club quietly. It was a long ride home that night. I began to understand that other people really didn't know how to deal with a casualty of war. They overcompensated, either by effusive praise or complete silence.

It was a similar experience at home. After the glow of my homecoming cooled, overcompensation was the order of the day. The natural, parental instincts to overprotect me emerged. Shouting arguments over little things intensified. Mom and Dad didn't know what to do or what not to do for me.

I began overreacting by demanding my way. "Get me a Coke!" "Help me with this tie!" If my parents didn't move fast enough, I'd get angry. Then I'd feel ashamed.

One day I learned that Elmer's wounded son was already dead and buried when I had been blatantly assuring his grieving father that, "Yes, he's going to be all right."

I stormed at my parents, "Can't anybody tell me the truth anymore?"

"We didn't want to hurt you, Max," was their tearful excuse. "We just wanted to spare you more pain."

With a grunt, I wheeled over to my stereo and turned it up loud.

Early in August, I flew back to Washington and Walter Reed. As I watched the checkered fields of Georgia drop away beneath the aircraft, I realized I couldn't go home again and fit in like I had in the past. I had changed too much.

11

FOUR FEET TALL

"We must not just do our best. We must do whatever it takes."

— Winston S. Churchill

There must have been a dozen of them. The doctors and therapists were all seated in a semicircle in the Walter Reed physical therapy clinic when I was called up for evaluation. All were there in their white uniforms—the heads of therapy and especially the chief of orthopedics, Colonel Metz.

The time had come for a decision in my case. I could feel my heart beating in the ends of my stumps.

Colonel Metz shifted in his chair and began: "You've come a long way, Max, in four months. You've healed nicely, and your skin grafts have taken well."

He smiled. "And from what I hear, you're gaining your strength back. The chief of occupational therapy reports that you've learned to use your new arm rather well. The chief of physical therapy tells me that your stumps are stable enough now to try a fitting for limbs."

I straightened in my chair. This was what I had been

fighting for all these months.

"However," continued Colonel Metz, "it's my opinion that you need more time in training."

What's he driving at? I looked at them all, a little uneasy.

"I think you need an intermediate phase to better prepare you for larger limbs later," he said. "I want you to think about wearing 'stubbies' for a while."

I had no idea what he was talking about. I wanted to try on a pair of the lifelike, flesh-colored legs I saw other amputees like Carl Nunziato wearing.

Colonel Metz saw my bewilderment.

"Stubbies don't look pretty," he said. "They're made of balsa wood and will fit on your stumps like a set of holsters. A pelvic belt around your waist will help to hold them on."

His eyes bored into mine. "You'll stand only about four feet tall. You'll have no knees, and instead of shoes you'll have wooden rockers to keep you from falling over backwards. Think of them as trainers for limbs later." The colonel now leaned forward. "Captain Cleland, these stubbies won't do your ego much good. But it's our conclusion that you should try them before we go to regular limbs."

"I'm willing to try anything, sir, to get going," I said.

"Good," said the colonel rising from his chair. "I'll order the limb shop to get started right away."

When I arrived at the hospital limb shop a few days later, it sounded like a factory. The whirring of lathes and the grinding of flywheels made my ears ring. Technicians in heavy, protective aprons stood at workbenches hammering, grinding, and sanding arms and legs in all sizes and in two colors—flesh white and flesh brown.

One of the limb-makers looked up and motioned me over to

a quiet corner. He introduced himself as Jim Cloud. Jim was an amputee who had lost a leg above the knee. He had become so fascinated by the limb-making profession that he had decided to make it his own.

All my questions about wearing artificial limbs spilled out.

Jim shook his head. "You'll never be completely comfortable in them. The best you can hope for is a good close fit and your stumps holding up."

My illusions about striding comfortably about on artificial legs were slowly being destroyed.

In a week I came back to try on my "stubbies." When Jim pointed to them, I blanched. They stood on the floor— grotesque, squat things. I couldn't believe they were to become a part of my body. They looked more like something from a medieval torture chamber.

"You'll have to sit down here," Jim said, pointing to a chair. Before helping me into it, he straightened his own artificial leg by cocking it so he wouldn't bend his mechanical knee and fall.

As I perched on the chair he handed me a pair of heavy, five-ply, woolen stump-socks. "These are to protect your stumps."

Jim and his helper slid them on. They fit snugly around the entire leg, but I felt like I was putting on a wool coat without any underclothes. With the sock on, there remained a roll at the top which cushioned the edge of the leg socket against my crotch.

I stared at the stubbies' awesome wooden holes into which I was to be poured. The holes looked small, and the shiny steel braces on either side seemed threatening.

"Grab around my neck," said Jim, "and let's see how these things fit."

I grabbed his neck with my good arm and an aide's neck with my right shoulder. Then I slid off the chair, straining to aim my stumps into the two wooden cocoons.

For the first time in five months, I was standing erect! My first sensation was a tremendous itching. "My God, it's driving me crazy," I gasped.

"Your circulation is coming back," said Jim. "It's all those nerves and little blood vessels. Your skin is now under pressure, but you'll get used to it after a while."

I stood gritting my teeth. *This was no rehabilitation exercise*, I thought. It was torture. I looked at the ugly chunks of balsa wood with their steel braces and the heavy leather belt around my waist. How could anyone walk in these things? *No way*, I thought. *No way.*

"The itching is killing me!"

"Take it easy," soothed Jim. "The blood will get down there in a minute. Now, just hold still, and let us adjust these braces."

As he worked, Jim explained the mechanics of my walking.

"First, you'll have to lean forward a little. Otherwise, you'll topple backwards because you have no knees to maintain your balance. Got that?"

I nodded.

"Secondly, as an AK (above-the-knee amputee), you rest your weight on your buttocks because that's where the pressure of your body is. An AK does not walk or bear weight on the ends of his stumps as does a BK (below-the-knee)," he explained. "Third, an AK walks primarily with his back muscles, not his leg muscles."

He patted the stubbies. "For you, it's all back and hips—if you can do it."

The two men carried me across the room and placed me between two parallel bars.

"Now, hold onto one bar and swing one leg forward," Jim coaxed. "Then, rock onto the other side and bring the other leg forward. You'll walk," he added, "as long as you stay between the bars."

I couldn't help but think of a toy I had as a child—a little wooden soldier with stiff legs swinging on pivots. When you placed him on a sloping board, he would wobble his way to the bottom in jerking steps.

The bars were not quite wide enough or high enough. When I rocked trying to swing a leg forward, I banged into them. Standing now four feet high, I had to dodge the parallel bars with my head at every step. Finally, rocking and swinging like the little wooden man, I made it to the end of the bars.

Breathing hard, I hesitated for a moment. Then, swinging around and staring at Jim with fierce determination, I made my way back.

I hung onto the bars, panting, sweat running down my face and body, my stumps itching horribly. I thought for a minute and then decided to try something. I rocked away from the bars at arm's length and then let go.

I stood erect, alone.

"Aha!" I chortled. "I can do it!"

"I'll be damned," exclaimed Jim.

I tried to take a step forward, promptly lost my balance and toppled head first. I caught myself by stiff-arming the floor and, in an instinctive reaction, made a push-up motion and shoved off the floor, rocking back upright.

Ablaze with pride and joy, I began to waddle around the limb shop showing off before the other workers.

I was nearly beside myself. I had accomplished what, to the onlookers, seemed virtually impossible. I had walked on stubbies unassisted the very first time. My stumps were on fire and my crotch burned fiercely, but my pride was beginning to heal. I was only four feet tall, but I had surprised the experts. I had beaten the odds. I was walking on the first thing they gave me. I was walking on the first day. What did they think about that!

After the two men removed the stubbies from my reddened

stumps, Jim said they needed some adjustments. "Come back next week, and we should have them ready for you."

I got back in my wheelchair which now seemed very old-fashioned and thrust my way out of the limb shop with a flourish. *I knew I could do it,* I told myself as I headed down the crowded hallway to lunch. *I knew I could do it.*

For the first time since I had entered Walter Reed in April 1968, I was really excited about my progress. I had healed up, gotten my strength back, been out in the world a little, and regained some confidence in myself. Now, in October, after six months of therapy, I felt that anything I wanted to accomplish was possible. I had had a taste of success, and it felt great!

After a few weeks of practice on the stubbies, I showed off my ability to the doctors. When they made their ward rounds, while most other patients rested in their beds, I stood proudly at the foot of my bed. Standing four feet tall on balsa-wood legs buckled at my waist, I was dressed in oversized gym shorts and a T-shirt, my flesh-colored plastic, right arm-hook—strap and all—exposed to view. I felt I had done well. Now, I wanted them to know that I was ready for the next step.

But there would be no next step at Walter Reed Hospital.

"You mean I'm being discharged?" I was incredulous when the chief medical officer gave me the news. He explained that I was to be discharged from the Army and moved to a Veterans Administration hospital.

"But nothing has been done yet to fit me for real artificial legs," I protested. Then I remembered something. Back in those groggy days when I first entered Walter Reed, I had indeed said I was willing to go to a VA hospital if it meant my getting home sooner. My future was sealed. Even while I had been learning to walk on my stubbies, preparation was underway to send me to the Veterans Administration.

That night, unable to sleep, I thought about all the other amputees who had stayed on here until they got their limbs and then were either retired or discharged from the military. It was obvious to me that a triple-amputee was not regarded as a "normal" amputee. My rehab program was seen as "long term." Such cases were to be sent to the VA.

At least they gave me a choice of Veterans Administration hospitals. I chose the one in Washington, D.C., rather than Atlanta near my home. I had two reasons for this.

First, I wanted to be away from home. I knew that rough times lay ahead, and I did not want my family and friends suffering along with me as I went through rehabilitation. From what had already transpired, I knew that trying to regain any sense of independence and personal dignity would mean a lot more agony. I would be fighting for my life as I wanted to live it.

Secondly, I wanted the best rehabilitation program that the VA had to offer. From my Washington experience, I assumed that the District of Columbia VA hospital would be one of my better choices. How wrong I was.

After three and a half years in the United States Army, my departure was unceremonious. It involved the normal round of paperwork. My photo was taken and stuck on my military retirement identification card. I compared it with the prewar photo of my old Georgia driver's license. I seemed to have aged 20 years. What a sad ending to the military adventure I had sought so eagerly.

It was a dismal, December day when I said good-bye to my buddies in the Snake Pit. They were all gathered together: No-Way Dave Alligood, out of his cast and looking forward to a family; Joanna-of-the-bedpans, who asked me to go fishing with her on my next pass; Big Harry, who welcomed me into the

Snake Pit that first night; and Carl Nunziato, finally leaving the hospital on his new legs, and ready to go to law school.

Major Julia Baker hugged me to her ample bosom and gave me a big kiss. I kept finding something in my eyes and finally turned my head.

"Don't let those b—ds get you down!" I heard Nasty Jack shout as I left the ward. An ambulance waited for me outside the same hospital emergency entrance through which I had been carried in the spring. I sat in the front seat of the ambulance feeling depressed and abandoned.

It is a short, 15-minute ride from Walter Reed to the Washington, D.C., VA Hospital. "How much can one person take?" I muttered gloomily.

I was soon to find out.

Max Cleland, age 6 months.   Max Cleland, age 4.

Max, working on Capitol Hill in Washington, D.C., meets Georgia's
senior U.S. Senator, Richard B. Russell, in 1965.

As an Army second lieutenant, Max is selected to serve as Aide de Camp to the Commanding General of the Army Signal School, Brigadier General Thomas M. Rienzi, Fort Monmouth, N.J., 1966.

Max serving as a signal officer with the First Air Cavalry Division in Vietnam, 1967.

Joe Goldstein

War casualty, the Snake Pit, Walter Reed Army Medical Center, Washington, D.C., 1968.

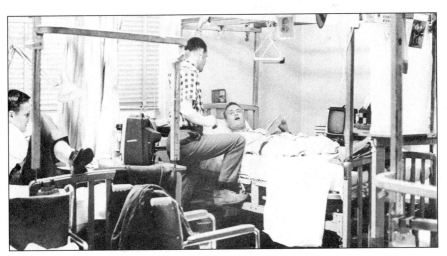

"Nasty Jack" Lawton and Max discuss life in the Snake Pit at Walter Reed Army Medical Center, Washington, D.C., 1968.

Betty Lyon

Max campaigning for the Georgia State Senate wearing his artificial limbs.

Jessie Sampley

Max as a newly elected Georgia State Senator, 1971.

Max Cleland: "The strengthening process still continues."

Max Cleland, with his parents by his side, is sworn into the United States Senate by Vice President Al Gore.

Senator Cleland and fellow Vietnam Veteran Senator Bob Kerrey.

IN HONOR OF ALL WHO SERVED

IN MEMORY OF THOSE
WHO MADE THE
ULTIMATE SACRIFICE
IN THE NAME OF FREEDOM

Richard Flo
Burnham

Flo

Joe Sports

Senator Cleland in front of the Vietnam Memorial
in his hometown of Lithonia, GA.

Max Cleland and David Lloyd, friends for life.

12

INTO A VETERAN'S WORLD

"If you can conceive it and believe it, you will achieve it."

— NAPOLEON HILL

"Here we are." The ambulance driver pointed to a white building looming before us on Irving Street, its upper floors lost in the gray mist. We swung into the driveway leading to the emergency room.

At the entrance, he turned off the engine and pulled my wheelchair out of the back. I was glad to have it with me. I figured it would take a while to obtain a chair through the Veterans Administration, so I had talked an old Army sergeant in the "pit" into letting me borrow one until mine came through.

I was wheeled into the emergency room and pushed to a reception desk presided over by a stoic-looking woman. "What's your claim number?" she barked.

Claim number? No one had told me about that.

"Wait over there." She pointed to a corner and picked up a phone.

It was quickly impressed upon me that in the hospital system of the Veterans Administration a patient is known by his "claim" number, not his rank or branch of service. The word, I discovered, came from the fact that a veteran has to "claim" a wound or injury. If the VA authorizes medical care, the veteran is admitted to the hospital or given attention on an outpatient basis. If the injury is the result of military service, a veteran supposedly gets priority treatment.

My priority treatment this day resulted in a two-hour wait after which an attendant handed me a pair of light green pajamas.

"You're going up to your ward now," he said. "You are to take no clothes, no personal effects, no food, no TV, and no radio up there. Understand?"

I nodded, wondering if I had been dropped off at a federal prison by mistake.

An elevator carried me to a higher floor where I was wheeled into a large ward and pushed up next to an empty bed. I was stunned. Most of the men in the ward were 20 or more years older than I.

Some stared at me like I was a man from Mars. Others blinked a couple of times and rolled over on their beds. It was obvious that these men had not the slightest inkling of what service in Vietnam had been all about.

Within two and a half hours of leaving Walter Reed, I had been stripped of rank, denied the amenities to which I had been allowed at another government hospital just up the street, and given no identification except for a number.

I was scared. I had come here to get rehabilitated, but it felt as if I had been sentenced to an old elephant burial ground. I expected the VA to be different but not this different.

Someone touched me on the shoulder, and I looked up.

"The ward nurse wants to see you," said the aide. As I rolled into her office, an attractive young black woman nodded to me and asked, "Mr. Cleland, what are you here for?"

I stared at her, not knowing whether she was serious or not. "I'm here to get fitted for artificial limbs," I finally managed.

She nodded and filled out several forms. A day or two later I was transferred to a smaller room on the ward with three other Vietnam veterans. I immediately began to feel better.

A heavyset, dark-haired woman stepped briskly into our ward late one afternoon and introduced herself as being from the social work service. I had heard these people were on the staff to help patients adjust to their new surroundings, find out about their families, and learn how the VA could help.

After pulling a card from her briefcase, she asked my name and some basic facts which she quickly wrote down. Looking up, she asked, "Now, what do you need?"

"Well," I answered, "I . . . uh . . . I don't really know. I just got here and. . . ."

She stared blankly at me for a moment, wrote something on her card, slipped it back into her case and stood up. Glancing at her watch, she said, "Well, I must be going." As she started to leave, I felt I had to find out more. Surely, she had some advice for me. As she hurried down the hall to the elevator, I propelled my wheelchair along behind her. My mind raced as I considered what to ask. I couldn't think of anything.

As the elevator door slid open, she got in and turned to face me. I looked up at her. "Uh . . . uh, what advice do you have?" I asked desperately.

She hesitated as the elevator door began to close. "Well," she said, "my advice is to stay out of the city at night. There's a lot of crime on the streets, you know." The elevator door squeezed shut, and I never saw her again.

After a few days' evaluation, the PT staff decided that because of my added weight, it would take a pretty big therapist to help me. I was turned over to Jon Peters, who stood more than six feet tall and was 230 pounds of sinew and muscle. I called him Big Jon.

It was the beginning of a lifetime friendship. Jon sensed my despair and kidded me out of my low moments. As he helped me on with my hated stubbies, he would wink. "You get around faster with these than some of the doctors."

Thanks to Jon's calming efforts, my steaming frustration didn't boil over. But I clumped unassisted up and down the hospital corridors to get attention and make a case for a decent set of limbs.

"The trouble with us, buddy," another ward mate told me one day, "is that you and I are combat casualties. The VA doesn't know what to do with us."

Until now, I had thought the VA hospital system had been established for patients like me. Yet it did seem that we were out of place. Older veterans populated the hospital. For a while, I resented these men being able to walk around in their VA robes with all limbs intact. I resented their being able to take a drug or a pill for their problem while I had to work on mine daily through sweat and pain. Later, as I began to understand what war does to people, I developed a different opinion about my fellow veterans. Some of the deepest wounds we suffer in life are not visible.

During my first weeks as a patient I began to check on more parts of the hospital, which was a large and fairly new facility. A recreational area with ping pong and pool tables and even a bowling alley was located on a lower floor. One afternoon I thought it would be nice to go down there for a little ping pong.

When I rolled into the recreational area, it was empty. A man who seemed to be in charge was turning out the lights.

"Hey," I said, "I came down to play a little ping pong."

He glanced at me, continuing his work. "Sorry, buddy, we're closing up."

I was dumbfounded. At Walter Reed, the Red Cross hall was open until 11 or 12 o'clock every night and patients could go there any time of the day to play pool or ping pong, eat cookies and drink lemonade or just visit with people.

Here it was 10 minutes after four and the recreation area at the VA hospital was closing. "Don't you open in the evening?" I asked.

"Nah," he answered, "we go home at 4:15."

This was the very time that patients were relaxing from therapy and getting out of their beds to enjoy a little recreation.

"But why don't you stay open in the evening?" I asked.

"Sometimes we do, on special occasions, but not all the time. We don't have enough staff," he grunted as he turned out the last light.

One day, Jon Peters made the suggestion that was to change my whole lifestyle. Tired of hearing my complaints about the shortages and inefficiency in the hospital, he said casually, "Why don't you get your own apartment?"

"What did you say?"

"Why don't you get your own apartment and become an outpatient here?"

"They'll allow me to do that?"

"Sure. If you can take care of yourself."

My mind began racing in a new direction. Why not? I ticked off my progress toward self-sufficiency: feed, dress, bathe myself—no problem there. The wheelchair gave me mobility. Elevators and ramps would enable me to get in and out of an apartment. Cabs would take me back and forth to the hospital for therapy.

In a way, I was being shoved out of the nest. But suddenly I wanted it. It was time to see what I could do out there alone in the world.

I rented a tiny, furnished, studio apartment on 16th Street near Walter Reed for $115 a month. I had my stereo shipped up from Lithonia, added some extra furnishings and moved in.

I adapted to apartment living sooner than I expected. In the morning, I'd slide to the end of my bed, reach out and grab the left armrest of my wheelchair, steady it and jump into it backward. Then I'd unlock the brake and propel myself into the bathroom. Since the chair wouldn't go through the narrow door, I'd hop onto a stool with coaster wheels. Pushing off the sink, I'd scoot to the tub where I'd perch on its edge and grab a handle above the soap dish to stabilize myself. Bracing with my left arm and right stump and leaning on the tub, I'd slowly let myself down into it. After my shower, I'd reverse the procedure. With a hefty pushup, I'd propel myself out of the tub, then onto the toilet seat and back onto my coaster stool. Back in my chair, I'd wheel over to my bed where I'd dress.

On Valentine's Day 1969, I had a housewarming party for my old buddies from the Snake Pit and some of my friends in D.C. We mixed drinks and turned up the stereo. For the first time in many months I felt almost ebullient.

We told lots of stories, lots of lies and reminisced about life in the "pit." We laughed about the time four amputees from our ward were out riding in a car which one of them had bought and learned to drive. A tire went flat on 16th Street during rush hour. They had all piled out—none with a good leg to stand on—to change the tire. One guy on crutches directed traffic around the stopped vehicle, another in a wheelchair supervised the other two who worked on the wheel.

Passersby on the sidewalk and in cars saw the crutches and wheelchair and thought there had been a terrible accident. Traffic was jammed for blocks.

The party also allowed us to catch up on the latest news. Someone yelled over to me. "Hey, Max, did you hear what happened to Nasty Jack?"

"No," I said, reaching over to turn down the stereo.

"Well, he finally got rid of that cast, but that hand of his was still a little palsied. So they sent him to Fort Benning to continue the healing process and attend the infantry officers advanced course. But instead of doing what he was told, he pulled all the bad medical stuff out of his records, got on a phone to Washington, and volunteered for a third tour in Vietnam!"

"That jerk," I said, shaking my head. I sat staring into my drink, thinking how this wiry, bright-eyed, profane friend had blasted me out of my gloom that first morning in the "pit." I had come to love that guy.

Later, Jack sent me a paperback book from Vietnam about a World War II fighter pilot who had been an ace for the British in the Battle of Britain. The pilot had lost two legs before the war, yet had fast become a legend in the Royal Air Force. His name was Doug Bader and his story, *Reach for the Sky*, was a great lift to me. I knew if Bader could do something that spectacular with no legs, I could certainly do something worthwhile with my life.

13

SIX FEET TALL

"The me I see is the me I'll be."

— Dr. Robert Schuller

A drizzling, winter rain beat on my apartment window when I awoke. I lay there not wanting to get up. For weeks I had been going through the same, boring routine of therapy, and I saw nothing ahead. Then I remembered. There *was* something special about today. I'd be going into the swimming pool for the first time.

I washed, shaved and dressed, then wheeled out my door. I took the elevator down to a coffee shop in my building where I usually ate breakfast.

At the hospital, I went to the physical therapy area where, with much grunting and gasping, I removed my street clothes and wrestled into a T-shirt and my size 50 boxer shorts. Then I got on my stubbies and clumped up and down the hospital halls for a couple of hours to strengthen my muscles.

At noon, I hit the chow line, which was now a bummer for me. I was overweight and my doctor had put me on a diet.

Furthermore, lunchtime conversation was often with outpatient men who were there for psychiatric treatment. Being on medication, they were usually spaced out.

After lunch came occupational therapy, where I had been constructing a small ceramic chess set. But today was different. I wheeled myself to the hospital's beautiful, indoor, heated pool. The pool area was warm and humid and resounded with the splashing and yelling of men playing volleyball in the water. A corrective therapist, a young, athletic-looking black guy, ran the program. He introduced himself simply as "Branch."

As he set me into a special chair on a ramp that sloped into the pool, all the old swimming sensations came back to me. I had competed in high school swimming meets and during one summer had served as a lifeguard.

I squirmed off the chair into the water—and sank like a bowling ball.

Panic hit me. Instinctively, I kicked my feet to rise to the surface. There were no feet. Branch's strong arm pulled me to the surface as I started coughing and spitting.

"Here," he grinned, "we've got something to keep you afloat." He took two one-gallon plastic Clorox jugs that were tied together and, with the rope between them under my arms, I floated.

Soon, I learned to do more in the pool than just float. I learned to kick my stumps and, sweeping with my left hand, found that I could even control my movement in the water. In the shallow end, I could discard the Clorox bottles and do something I hadn't done since my accident. Buoyed by the water, I could stand erect on my own. I could appreciate that marvelous sense of independence Franklin Roosevelt reported he felt when he was able to stand in the waters at Warm Springs, Georgia, during his illness.

Little victories like this kept me going. Soon I got down to one Clorox bottle. When I began experimenting with my breathing, I discovered that if I held my breath, I could float by myself. Next I found that I could tread water with my left hand. Then, synchronizing my breathing with hand movements, I learned to propel myself a bit. One day I developed a modified, one-arm breaststroke. With some practice, I swam the length of the pool. Before I left the hospital, I swam 20 laps—nearly a quarter of a mile—without stopping.

As my self-image began to rebuild, I tried to expand my social life.

I was told of a young woman who lived in my building. "She has an apartment right below you. Why not give her a call sometime?"

"Does she know about me?" I asked.

"No. But she's a warm, friendly person."

Sitting in my little studio apartment, I picked up the phone and held it for a long time. Summoning courage, I dialed her number.

"Hi," I said, "I'm Max Cleland. A mutual friend suggested that I give you a call. I live just above you here in the complex."

We talked for a few minutes. Then she invited me down to have a cup of coffee.

I hung up the phone in a state of excitement. Self-doubt rushed in. What would she think of me? Perhaps I could take her a little gift. Someone had given me a large sack of grapefruit. Grabbing three of them, I placed them in my lap and wheeled out of my apartment.

I rolled off the elevator, wheeled up to her door and knocked. A beautiful dark-haired girl opened it.

"Max?" she said, looking down at me. I reached up to shake her hand and the grapefruits in my lap all spilled onto the floor, rolling down the carpeted hallway.

"I'll get them!" I exclaimed.

"No," she protested, "let me do it." In our sudden efforts we almost collided. It was an embarrassing situation, but when it was over, both of us were laughing. The ice had been broken.

All of my therapy, especially my work on the stubbies and in swimming, was just preparation for my great dream: walking on limbs. The boost I received from learning to swim prompted me to force a showdown with my rehab supervisor. I insisted on a fitting of limbs. Finally, she gave in and set up a conference with representatives from three private limb-making firms in the Washington area. The three men examined me and discussed my capabilities.

Two of the men shook their heads. "I don't think he'll ever learn to walk," one said. "Too hard to fit."

"The effort wouldn't be worth it," commented the other.

Panic stabbed me. Was I being abandoned? Desperately, I looked at the third man who had been silent.

"I'll take him," he said quietly.

This man had been a therapist at Walter Reed Hospital and just recently had gone into a private limb-making business on his own. His name was Jack. He needed the business and was willing to take the risk.

My rehab supervisor, with her eye on her budget, did not request a set of new, plastic limbs with the latest in hydraulic knees. Instead, she ordered old-fashioned, wooden limbs which were bulky and hard to handle. They had swing-lock knees that could buckle on you and cause you to fall.

I sat there in the wheelchair, the copy of the order trembling in my hand, my thoughts a tangle of frustration. *Blast it all!* I could try to fight the situation. But then I thought it over. Perhaps I was being given a message. If I was going to learn how to walk I would have to do it in the toughest way. This could be the only shot I would have. Outdated limbs or not, I would learn with whatever they gave me.

The day finally came when the limbs were ready. I took a long cab ride to Jack's shop in Bethesda, Maryland, for an initial fitting of my first set of artificial limbs. It was March 1969. Almost a year had gone by since the grenade had blown off my legs.

When I wheeled into his shop. Jack steered me to his work room. "Those old-type wooden limbs aren't right," he said, "but we'll do the best we can for you."

The fact that Jack did not try to con me into thinking that I was getting the best made me feel better. The guy was honest. I also felt he was my friend.

The legs looked gross. Putty marks surrounded the hole where the steel brace had been inserted.

We moved to a set of parallel bars where I hung while Jack and an assistant struggled and tugged until the limbs were on. Next they fastened the leather pelvic belt around my waist. Jack made sure both knees were locked so I wouldn't fall.

"Ready?" asked Jack.

"I've been ready for a long time."

They lifted me up and edged back a bit.

I was absolutely terrified. I stood six feet tall again for the first time in almost a year. It was like looking down from the Empire State Building. I clung to Jack and his assistant, not wanting to move. Walking would be impossible, I felt. The heavy legs seemed to weigh a ton.

"How do they feel?" grunted Jack, wiping sweat off his brow.

"Terrible," I said.

"Where does it bite?"

"On my right side, Jack."

"Try and take a step or two to see if you can sink down in 'em a little more," Jack suggested.

I shook my head. "You've got to be kidding."

"Try it and see."

I hesitated, then took a step.

I took another. *Maybe it can be done after all*, my mind raced.

Crack! The wood on my right stump split at the steel brace.

"Blast it!" exclaimed Jack, "I was afraid that knot wouldn't hold."

"Knot? What knot?"

"The knot in the wood," Jack said shaking his head.

I sickened. Now, I'd have to be worrying about knots in the wood if my rehab supervisor at the hospital had her way.

"I'll have to bring them to you at the hospital in a couple of weeks," said Jack disgustedly.

"A couple of weeks?"

"Yes. It'll take that long to fix the things."

Two more weeks out of my life for a lousy knot.

I sat in my little apartment that evening listening to a late winter sleet drum against the window. My hope for a quick and simple fitting of artificial limbs was gone. The drama of being a battlefield casualty and the careful attention one received at Walter Reed was in the past. I felt like I was now a discarded warrior and an expense to my government.

I stared at my artificial arm lying in a chair, wreathed in plastic and leather straps. It was mainly for looks, serving no real purpose as yet.

Bitterness raged in me.

The sleet beat harder at the apartment window. I shivered, wheeled to the bed, grabbed a blanket and pulled it over my shoulders. I hunched under it sensing that a malaise was weakening me. The fibers of my emotional rope were snapping fast.

On Easter Sunday 1969, I awoke in pool of sweat. My head ached. Within hours they had me back in the Washington VA hospital. The doctors called it a flu virus. I was in no danger of dying, but I wanted to. I had looked forward to enjoying the holiday with some friends. But nothing was working out.

Most of the other men in my ward were visiting friends or families. As I lay there alone, the futility of my life bore in on me. What was I living for? To get myself together every morning to go through the pain, anguish, and humiliation of therapy just to do it again the following day? Weekends were reserved for drinking and trying to forget. I wasn't living, I was existing.

That Easter Sunday I was glad my ward was fairly empty for I sank into dark depression. In a deep wrenching of the soul, I lay in bed, convulsed with agonizing, gut-wracking sobs. I was bitter over the past. I was afraid of the future. And the torturous present seemed unbearable. I wanted to die.

Some might call this prayer. I don't think it was. I was not an atheist—but neither was the Lord a part of my life. The fact that He might have been reaching down to try and help me on His day of resurrection never entered my mind.

That evening I felt better. Somehow in those stark moments I found relief. Now, I felt free of false hopes, false bravado. I could live, or I could die. The choice was still up to me.

The ballroom was packed. It was in a hotel near Kennedy Airport in New York City. A large group of Vietnam amputees from Walter Reed and the Philadelphia Naval Hospital had been invited to New York by the National Amputation Foundation Chapter of the Disabled American Veterans. It was their spring banquet.

The "Amp chapter," as it was known, was largely populated by amputees from World War II. These World War II men and their wives were now reaching out to us Vietnam amputees.

Sol Kaminsky, a key officer of the Amp chapter, had extended an invitation to me. I found myself at a festive table.

One of the amputees told me about a guy named Sammy Neuzof who was soon expected. "You'd be interested in him, Max," he said. "Sammy was wounded in World War II and like you, lost both legs above the knee."

I was about to dip into my fruit cup when my dining partner nudged me. "Here comes Sammy now."

I looked up to see a nattily attired man walking into the ballroom. Trim, with styled, black hair, his dark eyes flashed greetings to the hellos called from the tables.

I couldn't believe it. This man *was* like me, and yet he looked great. True, he used a cane, and I could recognize the swinging gait—but his aplomb. Wow!

Moreover, on his arm was a shapely, attractive girl. "That's his wife, Annie," my friend whispered.

I stared at the two of them as they approached our table. We all were introduced, and I learned that Sammy and Annie had reared a family of two daughters. Still awestruck, I confessed to Sammy how much I admired what he had accomplished.

Sammy chuckled. "Look," he said. He leaned his cane against the table and walked a few steps. "You can do it, too," he grinned.

I hadn't had a drink but felt intoxicated. The orchestra struck up a fanfare and the master of ceremonies introduced all of us Vietnam vets one by one, a spotlight shining on each of us. Then the music started and soon the floor was filled with couples. One tall, red-bearded man, his entire right shoulder gone, was dancing with his wife. Men were dancing on crutches, some with legs missing, some even in wheelchairs. All seemed to be enjoying the evening.

The beat of the music got to me. Turning to one of the girls at our table, I asked, "Would you like to dance?"

"Sure," she smiled and together we went out on the floor. The music picked up and I swayed with the music in my wheelchair. My partner swirled around me, and soon I was swinging the chair around in time with the music. We both returned to the table, laughing and talking excitedly.

The others applauded. One of the men lifted a glass in salute: "To life, eh?"

I raised mine. "To life!"

Jack brought the wooden legs from his shop to the hospital after making the necessary repairs. Again I found myself suspended between the parallel bars.

"There," he said, after I was strapped into the legs. "They'll fit better now and bear your weight without cracking."

I looked down at them. They were still gross-looking things of wood, putty, and steel. But they held me up.

Big Jon walked with me at the start, holding my pelvic belt and staying at my side. The knees were still a problem. I toppled backwards once and would have split my head if another therapist standing by hadn't caught me. When I learned to lock one knee, I gained stability. I kept the other knee swinging freely.

But I was walking! And I was at my normal height again! Though I could walk without crutches, they urged me to use them most of the time.

When I went into a shoe store in downtown Washington, the clerk looked at my empty pant legs in bewilderment. I told him I wanted to buy some shoes.

"What size, sir?"

"Well, it doesn't matter much. I used to wear a nine and a half D."

He shrugged and found my size.

My socks were made of plastic.

At first, I could walk no more than the length of the hospital corridor. I gradually increased my stamina, and could feel my chest and shoulder muscles growing—so I knew I was getting stronger. One of my favorite trips was walking to a friend's office on the hospital's first floor.

One day this trip became a big test.

While seated on a chair in my friend's office, I attempted to get up. As I leaned on my crutch, its tip slipped on the slick tile floor, and I collapsed in a heap of leather, timber, and steel. My friend rushed to help but I waved him away.

A vision of the doctor at Walter Reed telling me I could never get up again flashed before me. With one knee locked, I used the leg as a brace and planted my foot on the tile floor. Then, balancing myself on the right crutch, I did a pushup with my left crutch. Groaning with effort, I slowly raised myself from the floor until finally I was standing again. Exhausted and drenched with sweat, I stood there in a flush of excitement.

Again, I had beaten the odds.

After several weeks, Big Jon hit me with a challenge: "Let's try going up and down the steps."

I felt that this was where I'd crash and burn.

The handrail was the answer.

Grasping it with my left hand, I lifted my left foot onto the first step and secured it with the instep. Then I swung my right foot up next to my left one. In this manner, steadying myself with the right elbow crutch, I brought myself up one step at a time. I practiced over and over. By the end of the day, I succeeded in taking an entire flight.

Now, the most difficult challenge awaited me. It was outside the hospital and took the form of a small, six-inch curb. That curb might as well have been the Berlin Wall. To mount steps I had a handrail. But out in the open I had no such stable object. It took me six weeks to learn how to negotiate that curb by myself.

When I finally mastered the curb, there was nothing left to

achieve at the hospital. According to the physical therapy department, I could now do it all.

On a sunny June day in 1969, 14 months after the grenade explosion, I walked across the front lawn of my home in Georgia for the first time in more than two years. I would never again feel the grass between my toes. But I felt good. My mother and father were poised in the doorway, grateful. I knew that I didn't need their help. I wouldn't ever have to depend on them again. Or anyone.

For a moment in the quiet afternoon, I stood there, listening to the faint summer sounds and catching the pungency of the honeysuckle growing along the granite wall.

I was sweaty from making the steps, and my legs were pinched and hurt a little, but I had grown used to the dull pressure and occasional nerve throb.

I was home again—on my own terms.

14

DRIVING A CAR

"Attitudes are more important than facts."

— DR. KARL MENNINGER

My next objective was to learn to drive a car. This dream had obsessed me all during my rehabilitation. Even in my darkest hours when I had lost hope of ever walking, I felt that somehow I would learn to drive.

During my stay in the hospital, I consulted several commercial limb and brace shops about driving. I usually drew blank stares. There were standard hand controls for legless people, but no one seemed to know what I could do with no legs and only one hand. "You need one hand to steer and the other to operate the gas and brake contol," a representative explained.

It was an ironic situation. I could get a grant from the Veterans Administration toward the purchase of a car, but at that time the VA did not have a nationwide program to teach a disabled vet how to drive. Congress passed such a program later, but in 1969 I was really on my own when it came to learning how to drive with but one hand.

Then I met Ralph Coley, another triple-amputee. We both had been Army captains in Vietnam, both had lost our legs above the knee and one of our arms just below the elbow. Ralph had stepped on a booby-trapped artillery shell. He had been sent initially to a VA hospital in Arkansas but decided to try the private rehabilitation center at Warm Springs, Georgia. Originally established for polio victims and later made famous by Franklin D. Roosevelt, the foundation's little machine shop had adapted a normal set of hand controls for the steering column of Ralph's car.

"They installed two small rings on a lever where I could grip the controls with the prongs of the hook on my artificial arm," he explained. He showed me how strong rubber bands provided a grip for the hook, allowing him to latch on securely to the lever.

"This way I can pull the hand control lever, activating the gas, and push it down for the brake. I steer with my good hand. It's a piece of cake!"

I was elated. As soon as possible, I went to Warm Springs and had the family Chrysler outfitted with the same controls. What a multimillion-dollar governmental rehabilitation program had failed to accomplish, a small, private foundation in middle Georgia achieved.

With the car back home and my parents watching proudly, I climbed in behind the wheel and took my first drive. After a half-hour test ride around Lithonia to make sure I had confidence, I headed for Atlanta that evening before the sun went down. My heart pounded at the thought of actually driving up to a night spot, getting out of my car, walking in and sitting down like a normal person.

A friend had recommended a small place on the east side of Atlanta. When I arrived there, I had trouble finding a parking place. Finally, I nosed the Chrysler into a space almost a block from the club. By the time I had wiggle stepped on my wooden limbs to the front entrance, my suit was soaked with perspiration. Three narrow steps led up to the entrance of the bar. They looked as imposing as Mount Everest. There was no handrail! With much grunting and straining, I managed. I entered the bar. It was so dark that when the waitress showed me my table and pulled out the chair for me, I almost missed it as I plopped down.

I sat there for a long time in the cool darkness thinking about the meaning of it all. When I had left Atlanta for Vietnam, I had hit most of the bars and dancing spots in town. I had danced myself to exhaustion. Now I was just grateful to be able to sit down in a chair without missing it.

It didn't take long that summer to put a lot of miles on my parents' car. I discovered drive-in movies, drive-in restaurants, and other spots which I found easy to handle. Little by little, I began to relax and enjoy myself.

One night, I made another major achievement. A group of us went to a nightclub in Atlanta. Drawing a deep breath, I turned to one of the girls and asked her to dance. Together we walked out on the floor and, while the band played, I moved and turned with the music.

Everyone had stopped to watch. When the music ended, the place erupted into applause. As I made my way back to my table, people came up and encouraged me. Later, as I was leaving the club, one man with a decided limp approached with tears in his eyes. "Mister," he said, "you don't know how much you helped me."

Although I would never be the person I once had been, I could now do some things most rehabilitation people hadn't expected of me.

I could walk.

I could swim.

I could drive.

I could dance.

I *was* getting strong at the broken places.

As my confidence grew, I began to feel more at ease. Of course, I always paid a price in pain and fatigue for my walking, swimming, driving, or dancing. And I could only use my legs for six hours or so. After that they were just too uncomfortable. But a whole new world was opening up for me.

Then came some unexpected help from my friends in New York. They referred me to the Veterans Administration Prosthetics Center there which specialized in amputee cases and which might give me a better fitting of limbs.

I grabbed the first plane for New York City.

In an old dilapidated building on teeming, noisy Seventh Avenue, I met Ralph DeGaetano. A single-leg amputee out of World War II, Ralph was a true artisan and an expert in limb-making. He threw away my old wooden limbs. Then working with the latest plastics, Ralph made two legs which fitted me perfectly.

"You'll still have to wear a pelvic belt and steel braces on your hips," he said, "but you'll find these limbs lighter, less bulky, and far more easy to handle."

On top of this, Ralph fitted my legs with the latest hydraulic knees. "A product of the space program," he said.

"Our man-on-the-moon project?"

"No," he grinned, "the German space program." To my blank look, he explained that the special knees had been designed by a scientist who had been part of the German rocket program in World War II.

I got more surprises at the prosthetics center. On one visit, I saw a young triple-amputee swing confidently into the center for repairs. He looked familiar. When he saw me he broke out in a wide grin.

"Max! How ya' doin', ol' buddy?" I stared openmouthed. It was the young guy who had ridden next to me in the ambulance in Japan. Not only had he gained in strength since I had last seen him at Walter Reed, but he was also walking. I found out in talking to him that he had gotten married and that he had found a job. *Incredible,* I thought to myself. *He's doing better than I am!*

Then I realized that if I had underestimated him, it would be easy for others to underestimate me. Slowly, it dawned on me how subtle the discrimination can be against disabled people in our society. One of the biggest obstacles to overcome is the negative attitude of so many who simply undervalue the disabled person and his potential to overcome his handicap.

On December 12, 1969, I stood outside a hearing room in the new Senate Office Building on Capitol Hill, nervously waiting for Pete Lassen, another disabled Vietnam veteran. The two of us were to testify about how the Veterans Administration was handling returning war veterans.

Pete rolled up in his wheelchair. As executive director of the Paralyzed Veterans of America, he had been working on the VA problem for many months. Pete was a neighbor of mine in my apartment complex and had invited me to tell the story of my rehabilitation struggle to a congressional committee.

I had agreed.

"How do you feel?" he asked.

"A little nervous."

"So am I," he smiled, swinging his chair toward the door. "Let's give it to 'em."

Together we entered the hearing room, I on crutches and Pete quietly rolling along beside me in his chair. We sat in the back.

Pete pointed to the large bank of TV lights focused on the long witness table in front of the room where we would sit.

"We're going to be on TV?" I asked hesitatingly.

Pete grinned. "Only if we say something interesting." After looking over the audience, Pete confided that those attending were from major veterans' organizations, the Veteran's Administration, and congressional staffs.

Senator Alan Cranston, a tall, lean, athletic-looking man in his 50s, strode into the room to chair the meeting. He had been a sergeant in World War II. With no waste of time, he banged his gavel to bring the meeting to order.

Witnesses were called before him to testify. The TV lights remained dark. The men and women in the press section looked bored.

As I listened to a World War II veteran give his viewpoint, I couldn't help but compare him to myself. He had been in "The Big War"—WW II. I had been in the war America had never understood. Our experiences had been sharply different.

The older veterans concluded their testimony. Senator Cranston then welcomed Pete and me as the next witnesses. The TV lights snapped on with blinding brilliance, and the cameramen quickly shifted into position. Pete pleaded for improved care of spinal-cord injured veterans, pointing out that in World War II, only three percent of the wounded came home in wheelchairs with spinal cord injuries, while in 1969, 31 percent of wounded Vietnam veterans coming to the VA had injuries to the nervous system.

The irony of the situation, stated Pete, was that it was VA doctors who developed techniques for keeping these men alive in the first place. But the hospitals served only the medical needs of these wounded and generally ignored their shattered emotions, he said.

Senator Cranston then turned to me. The TV lights felt hot on my face.

I told my story—the grenade explosion, the quick emergency care which saved my life, then the prolonged agony of rehabilitation. Modern medical techniques saved a lot of men on the battlefield,* I stated, only to complicate the rehabilitation and readjustment process back home.

"The returning wounded are not just the concern of one or two government agencies," I said. "They are the concern of the nation as a whole."

Nodding heads in the audience indicated agreement.

"The wounded Vietnam veteran is unique," I continued. "First, he is more likely to have a permanently disfiguring and disabling injury. Secondly, he is more likely to have doubts about the validity of his sacrifice."

The lights seemed to get hotter, and perspiration built up inside my shirt as I tried to sum up my feelings.

> "To the devasting psychological effect of getting maimed, paralyzed or in some way being unable to re-enter American life as you left it is the added psychological weight that it may not have been worth it, that the war may have been a cruel hoax, an American tragedy, that left a small minority of young American males holding the bag. The inevitable psychological depression after injury, coupled with doubts that it may not have been worth it, comes months later like a series of secondary explosions long after the excitement of the

* A July 24, 1969, *Wall Street Journal* article covered a U.S. Army report that showed an 81 percent survival rate for Vietnam wounded compared to 71 percent for World War II wounded.

battlefield is far behind and the reinforcement of your comrades in arms a thing of the past. And the individual is left alone with his injury and his self-doubts."

The hearing was well-publicized, and I began to receive mail because of it. The depth and compassion of the letters so touched me that I began to make more outside appearances. One was in a church near Atlanta.

Speaking to a Christian group made me uneasy. *I can't be phony about it and say it was faith and prayer that sustained me,* I wrestled mentally. I voiced my concern to those who had invited me, and they reassured me. "Just come and tell your story, Max."

So I did.

I told my story and then concluded, "God didn't make me to be just four feet tall."

15

THE COFFEE
STRATEGY

*"Politics is a lot like war except in war you can be killed only once.
In politics you can be killed many times."*

— WINSTON S. CHURCHILL

I was sitting in a comfortable chair at home in Lithonia, moodily staring out the window. It was a bleak January day with bare oak branches silhouetted against a gray sky.

The idea wouldn't go away.

The spark had first been struck in 1963 when I had gone to the Washington semester program. Ever since, I had dared believe that one day I would play some kind of role in government and politics. The spark had been stirred again during the congressional hearing.

As I sat in my chair, I shuffled some papers which listed the voting statistics of my county. My attention became focused more and more on my state senate district. It was a new district, having been created two years earlier by reapportionment. The incumbent was a Republican. I was a Democrat. But the incumbent had not established much visibility nor had he established much of a legislative record.

I analyzed a number of the district's precincts and their voting trends. Interesting. The district was like a pie slice with its tip composed of a few precincts in urban Atlanta. The slice extended outward through the suburban Republican belt into old rural townships which had been Democratic since Sherman had marched to the sea. It was a fascinating mixture of old and new South, including a 10 percent black population.

I reached for the phone and dialed my good friend and political mentor, Jim Mackay.

"I'm thinking about running for the state senate. When can I see you?"

A short time later I was climbing into my new, 1970 Oldsmobile. It was always the same; when I drove I felt like a human being again. I headed toward the county seat where Jim's law office was located.

Mackay, now in his early 50s, knew about both winning and losing. A former congressman from my district, he had lost his race for re-election in 1968 and was now out of office. I knew he would give it to me straight.

I pulled into the parking lot of his office building. After swiveling toward the passenger side of the front seat, I pushed open the car door, planted both feet firmly on the asphalt, put on my elbow crutch, pulled myself up by grasping the car door and locked my limbs. I walked into the professional building and rode the elevator up to his office.

Jim listened carefully as I explained my desire to be elected a state senator. We talked mostly about my mounting a campaign for the general election in November since it looked like I would be unopposed in the Democratic primary. No other Democrat was coming up against the Republican incumbent.

"You're sure you want to go through with it?" he asked.

"I'm sure."

Mackay, a Coast Guard veteran of World War II, leaned forward as his eyes bored into me. "I've got to tell you this. Running for public office is like combat—you can get shot."

"I know."

He warned me of the Republican tide that seemed to be sweeping the country, recommended that I contact members of the State Democratic Executive Committee for help and advice, then put me in touch with some of his former campaign workers.

"I'm with you," he said as he walked me to the elevator.

I drove home with a mixture of emotions. I was thrilled to have the support of my old friend, yet a little scared that now I was really on my own. I would be vulnerable—my name on the ballot, my reputation on the line.

The first step was to put my candidacy before the voters. That meant advertising and public relations. A friend suggested a small firm that was just opening up.

On a rainy spring afternoon, I drove to the house of Gus Mann. A thin, bespectacled man in his late 40s, he met me at the door and proudly showed me his shop. It consisted of one piece of typesetting equipment mounted on his dining room table.

I liked Gus. He was earthy, genial, and sharp. He pointed out that television was too expensive, radio didn't focus well on my district, and we could only run a few newspaper ads. So Gus began by putting together an eye-catching, hand-out brochure.

"What do you think?" he asked several days later as he handed me the layout.

"I think you're a genius."

My next step was to meet local Democratic Party officials. I drove to the local county office and knocked on the door. No answer. I borrowed a key and walked into a small, dusty, seemingly abandoned room.

All I could find was a little box of three-by-five index cards with names and addresses of some of the party faithful in my district. Most of the dog-eared cards seemed outdated. I salvaged some 15 names, stuck them in my pocket and left the office.

For the next few days, I sat at home trying to reach by phone or mail the names on the cards. I got nowhere. Frustrated and depressed, I abandoned hope of getting any real party support for my race.

Who would help me? Looking out my home window, I saw green sprigs coming out on the pecan trees and heard children playing in nearby yards. Then it struck me. I still had many school friends in the area. Perhaps through them I could put together an organization.

Running for office with no legs presented a problem. Normally, in a state legislative race, much of the campaigning is done on foot. Because I still felt undressed without my limbs, I believed that putting my best foot forward meant some kind of foot—even if it was made of rubber and plastic.

Hobbling up sidewalks on my crutches, I tried doorbell ringing. After the third doorbell, I had to rest in my car, exhausted. Then I tried canvassing homes in subdivisions where young volunteers were eager to help. They would knock on doors and hand out my brochure while I sat in the car and attempted to wave or smile. This also proved futile.

Shopping centers were a disaster. After entering the fourth or fifth store and having shaken 25 hands, I frantically searched for a place to lay down my crutches and sit.

Nothing seemed to be working.

After six weeks of this, it looked like my Republican opponent was going to win the November election by default. I felt there had to be a better way. I called a friend who was a Washington political consultant.

We did some talking on the phone, and one day when I was in Washington we got together over a cup of coffee.

"How about coffees?" Johnny said, looking down into his cup.

"What about 'em?" I said.

"I think you ought to have a lot of coffees, maybe one in every precinct," Johnny explained. "You can build your organization and increase your exposure at the same time without wearing yourself out."

He bit into a doughnut. "Coffees don't get you many votes, but they do identify people interested in helping you. Get them to hit the doorbells and shopping centers. Let *them* be your arms and legs.

"Get out into the neighborhoods," he continued, "drink coffee with the community leaders. Let them hear your story. You don't need a speech; just 10 minutes or so on why you're running and let it go at that.

"Then," he went on, pointing half a doughnut at me, "let *them* talk, let *them* react. See what *their* concerns are. After a couple of hours, if they aren't sold on you, they never will be."

Back in Atlanta, I remembered a Christmas card I had received the previous year from a housewife. She said she'd help me if I ever decided to run for public office. After fumbling through the cards which I had saved, I finally came up with her name. Belle. I got her on the phone, and we set up the first coffee for early June.

Belle invited friends and neighbors to her house. After a brief introduction, I sat down in a straight-back chair in her big, homey kitchen and looked directly into the smiling faces of about a dozen ladies. Stuffed with coffee and cookies, I felt relaxed and comfortable. Belle stood proudly at the door, waiting to refill empty coffee cups.

I told the ladies that one of my biggest hurts from the Vietnam experience was losing confidence in my own government. I then brought this down to our state level and pointed out that we had the nation's worst record in the number of high-school drop-outs.

"Any success I've had has been due primarily to my education in the public schools. But our state can do better, much better."

The ladies were with me. I quickly turned to their questions. Somebody asked about Vietnam.

"To be very blunt about it," I said, "we're trying to save face in Vietnam, and in the process we're losing our ass."

Belle's face turned white. There was a silence in the room. As I paused to sip my coffee, she asked me to come into the living room with her a moment. There, with tears in her eyes, she said, "I can't believe it. You've insulted all my friends. I just can't believe you've used such language in my house. These are good, church-going people here and they're not accustomed. . . ."

"Belle, if I said anything wrong in there, I'm sorry. I guess I just got carried away."

My first political "coffee" resulted in my writing each person a letter apologizing for my language and asking their forgiveness. At Belle's suggestion, I phoned some who were particularly offended. The language of the Army and hospital wards I had known for five years was not the language of hometown America. I was learning a lesson. I also learned that there was a lot of anger churning within me about Vietnam.

After cleaning up my language, I carried the race to my opposition in the Republican suburbs where the incumbent's strength lay. There were occasions for speeches and personal appearances, but by and large the campaign consisted of having coffees and enlisting volunteers to set up yard signs or getting them to work on telephone committees.

One of the few speeches I made in the campaign was not really a speech at all. It was an introduction. It came about because one of the contenders for the Georgia governor's race that year in the Democratic Primary had set up a local headquarters near my hometown. I was asked to introduce him at the gala opening.

A big wooden speaker's stand with red, white, and blue

bunting had been erected in front of an abandoned service station. It was a hot July evening. The candidate had on a white, short-sleeve shirt and a dark tie. After we met for the first time, I turned to some 200 people clad in overalls, sport shirts, and house dresses clustered around the speaker's stand and, after a brief introduction, welcomed the candidate to our county.

His name was Jimmy Carter.

Many of my high school classmates helped in my race. But there was one former classmate to whom I didn't listen. One hot summer afternoon after I had campaigned my way through a Lithonia shopping center, this friend stopped me at my car.

"Max," she said, "I'm proud of you, and you're going great. But there's one thing you're not doing."

"What's that?" I asked.

"You haven't given the Lord credit for your comeback."

I was annoyed but tried to give her a diplomatic answer.

She shook her head sadly. "I'm sorry, Max, but it's easy to see you're trying to do it all on your own."

I turned, shifted my crutches and swung my way back to my car. "I have done it on my own," I muttered angrily.

After eight months of campaigning, spending $10,000 and losing almost 20 pounds, I strapped on my limbs once more to go to my local precinct hall to vote on election day.

My parents drove me there. When we arrived, my campaign supporters and friends had already gathered around. Standing in the voting booth, I had to lean one of my crutches up against the wall to free my hand to mark the ballot. Then I climbed back into the family car and returned home, totally exhausted and relieved that the ordeal was finally over.

That evening, my parents and I went out to a nearby country club where we had rented a room for an election night party for some 200 volunteer workers, telephone committee members, precinct leaders, coffee givers, and contributors. We had several television sets scattered around and a scoreboard on the wall showing the precincts. A buffet supper was set up, and the band was just beginning to play when someone yelled, "Hey, returns from the first precinct are coming in."

We all clustered in front of the television sets. There was a loud, collective groan. Bad news.

"Don't forget," a friend encouraged, "that's a Republican stronghold."

As other precincts came in, the vote slowly began to turn in my favor. When Lithonia gave me 98 percent of its votes, a loud cheer arose and the band struck up a tune.

That evening, final returns showed me with more than 56 percent of the vote. At age 28, I would become the youngest member of the Georgia State Senate. I would also be the only Vietnam veteran in the senate.

The first week of January 1971, I stood on the floor of the Georgia State Senate with my left hand on the Bible and took the oath of office as a Georgia state senator. I had done what I had set out to do. I had learned to walk. I had learned to swim. I had learned to drive. I had learned to dance.

And now I had learned to run.

16

POLITICAL
WARFARE

"Politics is the art of sudden death."

— Pollster Lou Harris

The year 1971 was a dramatic time to be in Georgia politics. I had heard about the old politics of the Georgia legislature, about the wheeling and dealing of Capitol politicians for votes. I dug in my nonexistent heels.

But Jimmy Carter surprised me. In trying to make the most of his first and most popular year, the new governor pushed hard for reform and reorganization of state government—but in his own style.

Leading the opposition was the former governor, Lester Maddox, who was now the newly elected lieutenant governor. Since the lieutenant governor was also the presiding officer of the senate, this brought the storm center of Carter's reform effort and Maddox's opposition to my front door.

When the reform measure came up before the senate, tempers flew and tensions rose. As the moment of truth approached one day, Governor Carter called me and two other senators into his office for lunch. I went expecting some strong arm-twisting. Instead the governor leaned back on a couch and in a low-key, quiet way explained why the reorganization bill was needed for better state government.

I left his office perplexed by this man who was so straightforward and sincere about his proposals. He sure was different. He had made a believer out of me, and I decided to vote with him.

Amazingly, the Carter reorganization proposal passed the Georgia legislature, winning in the senate by one vote. The rest of Governor Carter's four-year team was spent fighting brush-fires scattered by his first and most important fight. During this time I gained a strong respect for Jimmy Carter. His mettle was often tested severely, but he never took his eye off his goal—a streamlined state government to serve people in a more eco-nomical and efficient way.

The more I watched him at work, the more I realized that here was a man who followed some inner, guiding light. This enabled him to take surprising risks. Though his soft-spoken style was often misinterpreted by the Georgia legislature, Jimmy Carter showed a single-mindedness of purpose and a persever-ance which I've never seen equaled in public life. The venerable Georgia secretary of state, Ben Fortson, who had been around Georgia politics for more than 30 years, was once asked to com-ment on Jimmy Carter.

"He's like a South Georgia turtle with his head up against a cypress stump," said Fortson. "You think that lil' ol' turtle can't move that big stump. But he jes' keeps pushin' and pushin', and before you know it, he's done it."

For the rest of his tenure as governor, Carter kept on his desk a model of a turtle with its head up against a cypress stump.

Meanwhile, the war in Vietnam was taking the lives of more and more Americans each week. It was time, I felt, to negotiate our withdrawal in exchange for our prisoners of war. Another disabled Vietnam veteran, state Representative Walt Russell, and I collaborated as to how we might jointly sponsor such a resolution.

Walt was a decorated veteran of the Korean War and had helped lead the First Air Cavalry Division to Vietnam in 1965. There he was wounded and spent a long period of rehabilitation in the States. A nephew of U.S. Senator Richard Russell, he had excellent political ties, and his distinguished military career earned him high respect in the Georgia House. Though we were both newly elected, Walt and I carried a unique credibility in regard to the war. When our resolution passed both houses of the legislature, the State of Georgia for the first time went on record for a pullout of our forces from Vietnam.

Walt and I had other unfinished business. He had taken a slug from an enemy machine gun in the back of his head. He had been left paralyzed on one side. We both had strong convictions that state government should lead the way toward better public facilities for handicapped people. We cosponsored Georgia's first legislation requiring new or substantially renovated public buildings built with public funds to be completely accessible to the handicapped. It passed the legislature and was immediately signed into law by Governor Carter.

The need for all buildings to be accessible to the handicapped had been driven home to me in a personal way during my first week as a state senator. I had been given the room number of my first committee meeting but couldn't find it. I was using my wheelchair that day and raced around asking attendants and doormen for the room's location. Though the 100-year-old, gold-domed statehouse had elevators, it also had a mezzanine reachable by stairs. This is where the meeting was being held. I ended up missing my first committee meeting. Ironically, it was the health and welfare committee which dealt with the problems of the disabled.

My problem with limited mobility grew as I campaigned for my second senate term in the 1972 election.

I had driven to a large utility company where I was to meet the employees during their lunch hour. The firm had invited all candidates to come and set up a booth and distribute literature.

It was hot that day and my leg stumps were already raw and burning from wearing my artificial limbs. However, I pulled up near the plant entrance and worked myself out of the car where I was met by a young girl who introduced herself as my hostess.

Together we walked through the entrance down a long corridor which seemed to stretch to infinity. After some distance, I asked, trying to keep from gasping, "Uh, how much farther is it?"

"Oh, not far," she said brightly, "there's an elevator at the end of the hall."

In the elevator I leaned against the wall, grateful for the chance to rest. At our floor, we stepped out, and she pointed down another long corridor. "It's there at the end."

We made it down the interminable hall, my hostess chattering cheerfully all the while. Finally, I lurched into the lunchroom and collapsed in a chair. I was so exhausted that my hostess and I ate lunch alone.

Lunch over and few voters in sight, my hostess and I proceeded to leave. We made it to the elevator where I caught my breath. I could feel little rivulets of sweat trickle down my stumps.

The elevator stopped, and we got out. Setting my jaw, I swung my body, step-clumping, down the long hall. We reached the end, pain shooting up my legs, my crotch on fire with abrasions from the sweat-soaked padding.

"Oh," said my companion, "I'm sorry. We got off at the wrong floor. We can't get out here."

Biting my lips and fighting to keep back tears, I managed to get back to the elevator. We finally made it to the entrance.

For half an hour, I slumped in my car trying to pull myself back together. But I couldn't rest any longer. I had to speak to a group of senior citizens at the county public library.

By now, three o'clock in the afternoon, a hot Georgia sun was bubbling the asphalt. I pulled up as close to the old library building as possible. Ahead stretched my nemesis— stairs. They led down to a basement meeting room where my audience waited.

I had to do it. *Thank heavens for the handrail*, I thought. Locking my knees so the limb was stiff, I lowered my leg to a step, gripping the rail. Then, using my crutch, I wrestled my other leg down to the same step.

The group waited patiently. I'm sure some of them had similar problems on stairs. After joining them, I talked for 40 minutes explaining why they should vote for me. After smiling nods and handshakes, I faced the steps again.

Back home, I fell on my bed completely exhausted. Mom gave a cry when she saw the ends of my stumps. They were bleeding. By now I knew I could not take the hellish torture of the pain I was putting myself through anymore. The next day, Saturday, my doctor confirmed it.

"Get off your legs, Max," he ordered, "until your stumps heal."

Somehow my machismo had been involved in walking on those legs. To hear him order me off them was a welcome relief. At least he had *told* me to do it. That provided some balm to my bruised masculinity.

On the following day, Sunday, I attended a coffee. It was the first time I had ever gone out campaigning without my artificial limbs. As I sat in the living room in my wheelchair, I felt completely relaxed and comfortable. I was able to answer questions better. Before, while struggling on my limbs, I began to get uptight after a half hour. Now, I felt affable and relaxed and was even able to attend another coffee across town later that afternoon.

Traveling alone with the wheelchair was fairly simple. To get into my car, I'd roll up to the passenger side, hop into the seat and "standing" on my stumps would grab the chair with my left hand and hoist it into the front seat. Getting out was just as easy.

The big wheelchair test came when I went campaigning one morning in a shopping center. I felt apprehensive and vulnerable, never before having rolled up to someone in my wheelchair to sell myself as a candidate. For some time, I sat in my car, afraid to get out. Finally, summoning courage, I lifted the chair out, slipped into it, and rolled across the asphalt toward the stores.

A man was walking to his car and I approached him. "Hi," I said, sticking out my left hand, "I'm Max Cleland, your state senator. I'm running for re-election this November. . . ."

"Sorry," he grunted, walking on, "I'm voting for the other guy."

I sat there feeling rejected, watching his back. Everything within me wanted to retreat to the sanctuary of my car and drive home. But I knew I had to keep going.

Forcing a smile, I turned my head and pushed my way closer to the stores. "Good morning, I'm Max Cleland, and I. . . ." On and on it went that morning. Many people responded favorably, and by noon I felt I had endured my baptism of fire. I spent the next three weeks fighting hard for votes because every poll indicated a nationwide sweep for the Nixon-Agnew ticket. It seemed very likely that I and every other Democrat in my county might be defeated.

On election night, my friends and supporters met in a room

we had rented over a bank in downtown Lithonia. Judging from early returns, my re-election prospects were dim. The Republicans were capturing everything in the county—from Congress to coroner. In the end I came on strong and squeaked through with 53 percent of the vote.

That election night was meaningful for me personally as well as politically. I had worn my artificial limbs to the victory party, thinking perhaps that since I wore them on my last victory they might bring me luck this time. Again my machismo was involved. I wanted to be "on my feet" so to speak, win or lose.

As I struggled up the stairs to the second floor room, the wife of Lithonia's mayor met me. She knew about my troubles with the limbs. "Max," she asked in concern, "why are you wearing those things?"

Then she put her hand on my arm. "We love you the way you are."

Later I thought about her comment. I needed to come to terms with the fact that *I* had to love me the way I was, too.

Except once when serving as best man at a friend's wedding, I never wore my limbs again.

During my second term as state senator, I became deeply involved in helping Vietnam veterans who were now returning to Georgia by the thousands. Many wanted to go back to school, but while World War II veterans received full college tuition, Vietnam veterans did not. A single vet going full time to school in the early '70s received only $130 a month.

Governor Carter got interested in the problem and in late 1972 appointed me to head a commission exploring the needs of returning Vietnam veterans. We held public hearings, received testimony, and conferred with state and federal officials.

Burt Westbrook, a friend and Vietnam veteran, came up

with an idea. "What if the state waived tuition for veterans going to its publicly supported universities?" he asked. "Wouldn't that in effect make their GI Bill money go further, attracting them back to school?"

It sounded good and I introduced it in the senate in the form of a bill. But to get the state senate to pass a resolution on Vietnam was one thing; it was quite another to get it to spend state money for Vietnam veterans.

We did get the bill passed in the state senate, but it was modified by the house. As finally passed by the Georgia legislature in 1974, the bill gave veterans special preference for state educational loans and grants. It was a pittance of my original proposal, but at least it was something.

That same year, the United States Congress passed dramatic increases in GI Bill education rates and extended the period of eligibility from eight to ten years. Since then, some 66 percent of eligible Vietnam veterans have used their educational benefits in one form or another, the highest participation rate ever in the history of the GI Bill.

After passage of the modified education bill, my last two years in the senate became more and more frustrating. A powerful senate leader came up to me on the senate floor one day and threatened that if I didn't support him in a special interest bill then on the floor, I'd never get another bill out of committee. I was sickened by his crass approach.

I did not support him, and as it turned out I never did get another bill out of committee.

By now the Maddox forces had completely consolidated their power in the senate, and Carter's popularity was waning. When we Carter supporters tried to change the rules in the senate so that we could capture more committee assignments, we lost. In political terms, I was now dead in the water.

My only alternative, as I saw it, was either to go up the

political ladder or step out of public office. But by now politics had become my life. After careful study, there seemed only one way to go.

Up.

17

ANOTHER LONG-SHOT ATTEMPT

"If you can make one heap of all your winnings
And risk it on one game of pitch-and-toss,
And lose, and start again at your beginnings,
And never breath a word about your loss . . ."

— RUDYARD KIPLING

Since Lester Maddox was running for governor in the 1974 elections, my best shot was to run for the post he was vacating—lieutenant governor. At that time, the lieutenant governor had much authority over the senate. He ran the committees, called up legislation, determined who sat on and chaired the committees and which bills went to committee. Running for this office was a long shot. But so was everything else I had attempted since the grenade shattered my body.

I began a year-long campaign in my wheelchair, competing against 10 other political hopefuls. The leader of the pack was Zell Miller, a former executive director of the state party. He quickly took the lead in the polls.

Another popular contestant was a young housewife, Mary Hitt. She had an engaging personality and a fine personal following. She quickly occupied the runner-up post.

I was undaunted. Hadn't I come out of nowhere to capture my senate seat? Didn't I win my re-election when many other Democrats were lost in the backwash of the 1972 Republican landslide?

My confidence had been bolstered in other ways. One way was in discovering that I could enjoy again one of my boyhood sports. At the time, I was dating a girl whose little sister had a basketball hoop above their garage door. One warm day I saw her and her friends shooting baskets.

"Hey, let me try one," I called. They threw me the ball. It felt good to be holding it. I thought of my old friend Edgar Abbott and his words: "No telling when you'll have to use your left hand."

I shot it toward the basket and it hit the garage door below, breaking a window. A great start! Still determined, I took another shot. That one missed too, but soon I managed to drop a few in the net. The old magic came back, and I was hooked. From then on I shot a basketball whenever I could and became good at it.

News photos of my shooting baskets in charity events made good copy for my campaign for lieutenant governor. I needed every bit of help I could get. Instead of one district, I now had to cover all of Georgia. It was exhausting physically, and financially draining. Yet I was soon speaking everywhere from tiny churches in small towns to executive luncheon meetings in Atlanta.

As the primary election day neared, my hopes rose with each passing day. After all, I had been a winner in almost everything I had attempted and against tough odds.

On election night, August 13, 1974, I became a loser for one of the few times in my life.

The victory party which had been scheduled in an Atlanta hotel ended early because there was no victory. When the returns came in, I had finished third—one percent out of second place and a runoff with the leader.

I had done my very best, had traveled all over the state for a year and spent $100,000. Now I was $20,000 in debt and out of a job.

It was a strangely shattering experience for me. Losing my legs and an arm had been an accident, I reasoned, but losing in my chosen field was a personal, humiliating failure. My identity and self-esteem were wrapped up in politics. With defeat, my psyche careened down into a dark hole.

As the weeks wore on, my phone remained silent. The reporters and TV people who had called so often before were not interested in me now.

I was a loser.

I couldn't shake it. I sank into self-pity. Then deep depression. My life seemed a total loss.

One morning as I leafed through the newspaper, I came across a story about a man I had known who had resigned a very fine position. The article reported that when people asked him what he was going to do now, he replied, "I don't know. But as they say, 'Let go and let God.'"

Let go and let God? *How weird*, I thought. How could anyone feel so serene about his future?

In struggling to escape my depression, I remembered that Senator Alan Cranston was running for re-election in California. We had kept in touch since his senate hearing, and I offered to fly out to the West Coast and campaign for him. He seemed delighted to have me and for some weeks I traveled throughout California, meeting veterans' groups and campaigning for the senator on radio and television.

In return, Senator Cranston came to Atlanta as guest of honor for a fund-raising dinner to help me pay off my campaign debts.

Some weeks later while on the telephone with one of the senator's aides, I learned that there was a staff opening on the senate veterans' affairs committee for someone to make on-site studies of VA hospitals. I flew back to Washington and applied for the job. Several weeks later when I was back in Georgia, I received the good news. The job was mine. It paid $12,500 a year.

Early one chilly March morning in 1975, I waved goodbye to my mother and father, wheeled myself to the battered Oldsmobile—now on its second hundred thousand miles—and dragged myself and my wheelchair inside. Mother handed me a brown paper sack bulging with sandwiches and a jug of iced tea.

I nosed the Olds out the driveway. In the mirror I could see my parents standing there. I waved out the window again, and turned onto the highway toward the interstate—driving north—headed for a moment in time that had been building up for almost 20 years.

18

ENCOUNTER ON
INTERSTATE 95

---

*"There's a divinity that shapes our ends,
Rough-hew them how we will."*

— SHAKESPEARE

It is 635 miles from Lithonia, Georgia, to Washington, D.C.—
interstate highways straight through—and I wanted to make it
by nightfall. Twelve to thirteen hours of steady driving would
do it. And it would give me a lot of time with my thoughts.

As I approached the Georgia-South Carolina border, I
thought of how many times I had left my home state and how
many miles I had traveled in recent years. I'd been halfway
around the world to Vietnam, and logged all those miles campaigning in Georgia.

For what?

Excitement?

Fame?

Prestige?

Power?

What drove me?

What had I been trying to achieve?

An ego trip to win trophies and medals?

Was my compulsive desire to go to Vietnam an effort to prove something to myself?

Was I searching for some impossible dream—or was I searching for myself?

The questions flew at me like the tar strips clicking under my tires. I had no answers for any of them. I knew only that I desperately wanted to feel better about myself. I had come to accept my disability to a certain extent, but I wasn't happy about my life. Even when I had been victorious in politics, I didn't have the joy that one is supposed to have. And defeat had sunk me to the depths of despair.

Why was I so insecure? The answer, I realized, had to involve something very basic within me.

A noon sun glazed on the interstate highway. I stopped at a roadside park and ate a pimento cheese sandwich. Mother had made these since I could remember, grinding the yellow cheese in a white mixing bowl and adding chopped pimento. How loving and understanding she and Dad had been to me all these years.

A sadness filled me as I turned back onto the highway. My thoughts roamed over my childhood days as I struggled for answers to the unrest in my spirit. I had grown up in a Christian home and believed in God. But exactly what was it that I believed about Him?

I started to push this thought aside as I had done so many times in the past. Then I checked myself. *Face up to it, Max. If you say you believe in God, where do you stand with Him?*

I stood nowhere with Him!

There it was—an honest admission. I had never pretended to be anything spiritually that I wasn't. I hated hypocrisy. I disliked piousness. I believed that God created me, sure, but He had given me a mind with which to think, to reason, to plan;

He had given me a body to develop and to train. He had given me the equipment I needed to make it in a tough world on my own strength. And I had done this.

I reviewed my accomplishments: high school awards, ROTC training, paratrooper school, aide to a general, fighting for life after the explosion; then making it back in the world as a triple-amputee. I had done it all on my own!

Then why was I so dissatisfied on the inside?

It was now late afternoon, and rain clouds darkened the horizon as I crossed the Virginia state line. I reached down and switched on my headlights.

Once again my mind drifted back through the years—back to when I was a tot and loved to escape my grandmother and run free in the outside world. That was the beginning of the drive for freedom and independence that had motivated my entire life.

Funny that it should pop into my mind now, but I remembered again those occasions in a small country church when the preacher had stirred me with his impassioned words. He had exhorted:

"Christ is your Savior. Follow Him. Obey Him."

Strange how those words returned to me now for they had not really penetrated my small boy mind. Or had they?

I thought about that for a moment.

Then a new thought struck me. I had shrugged off church attendance after high school as not important because I had so many other things to do.

Was this the reason I now felt so restless and unhappy in my spirit?

A new direction of thought opened up. I had been so full of pride over my ability to run my own life, but how well had I really done it?

I shivered. A sign indicated that Richmond was 80 miles ahead. Rain was splattering on the windshield. Back I went to my thoughts.

I had not only made the decision alone, against the advice of almost everyone, to volunteer for Vietnam, but I had also made a decision that I did not need God in my life. It was true.

I remembered the words I had read in the newspaper only a few months before: *"Let go . . . and let God."* I had never let go of anything I wanted in my whole life. Instead I wanted to be in control of everything. That's why those five words had so startled me when I first saw them. How could one let go and let God—and still be successful? I realized though that maybe this was faith—not a clutching, but a letting go! I had certainly not had that kind of faith in God. And so He had let me go my own way.

My eyes began to fill, and emotion surged through me. The tears burned as I strained to see through the steady beat of the windshield wipers.

"God forgive me! God help me!"

The words came out suddenly, a deep inner cry of my soul bursting through the controlling nature of my will.

Tears streamed down my cheeks.

Then something happened inside me. My racing heart suddenly slowed. The knot of tension and frustration began to dissolve. I could feel changes taking place in my physical body as a feeling of peace spread through every tissue.

Nothing was changed on the highway outside. Cars still sped by on the rain-slicked pavement. The windshield wipers beat their steady cadence. And the first mileage marker to Washington appeared.

But the glow within me remained. And with it came a revelation. Though I had departed from God, He had never abandoned me. Though I had ignored Him, He continued to love me. And now when I had reached out to Him, He came to me—right here on Interstate 95.

The rain was ending, and ahead I could see the lights of Washington glowing in the night sky. It was an opportunity for a new life.

I was ready—if He was.

19

OVAL OFFICE
REVISITED

---

*"Life is like a spiral staircase. We keep coming back to the same points,
but always from a different perspective."*

— WILLIAM BUTLER YEATS

It was early evening when I arrived at the home of our family friends, DeWitt and Winnette Buice. Before going to bed that night, they invited me to go to church with them the next morning. I quickly agreed.

As I sat in Clarendon Baptist Church that Sunday, March 2, 1975, I found meaning in every part of the service. I was alive to everything—the friendly greetings of the worshipers, the words of the hymns, the prayers, the reading of Scripture and the pastor's warm, reassuring message. When the service was over, for the second time in 24 hours, I admitted to myself I had a need in my life only the Lord could fill.

In March 1975, I started my job with the U.S. Senate Committee on Veterans' Affairs. At the beginning, I had to overcome bitter memories of my callous treatment at the

Washington VA hospital. I came on too strong at first with my criticism. I made mistakes. But gradually I began to learn about this vast government agency with its 230,000 employees serving more than 500 different facilities including 172 hospitals, 58 regional offices, 44 clinics, 88 nursing homes, and 107 national cemeteries.

The months passed. Jimmy Carter entered the campaign for the 1976 presidential election. When I learned that he planned to address several hundred students in the Library of Congress, I wheeled over to hear him.

The auditorium was hot, and the candidate removed his coat and spoke in shirtsleeves. How like that first time we met when he spoke in shirtsleeves to several hundred people gathered outdoors in front of a gas station!

After the speech he spotted me near the stage. "Max!" he shouted. He came over and gave me a hug. Then we reminisced about our time together in Georgia and talked about the campaign.

One summer afternoon in 1976, Senator Cranston's deep, warm voice was on the phone. He began by saying that he thought Jimmy Carter was going to be the next president. Then he asked me if I would consider being appointed as administrator of the Veterans Administration.

I was astounded.

"I believe you can do it," he added, and suggested that I think it over and get back to him.

After hanging up the phone I sat staring at it for a long time. *How could I ever handle anything like that?* But I gave it serious thought. Slowly I began to feel more and more confident about my understanding of this organization. By now I had spent almost two years dealing with some of its problems. Based on my own experience as a Vietnam veteran and as a patient, I felt I had developed a personal insight into how the VA could improve in certain areas. Perhaps I *could* provide the agency with some leadership.

Three days later I called Senator Cranston and told him I was interested and available for the job.

Jimmy Carter was elected president in November 1976. On January 19, 1977, the day before the new president was sworn in, Hamilton Jordan called and said the president would like to see me on inauguration day at four o'clock at the White House.

When I arrived at the White House, a secretary led the way as I rolled my wheelchair down a gold-carpeted corridor on the second floor of the West Wing.

The secretary stopped and pointed to a door on my right. I remembered. It was the entrance to the Oval Office. Two secret service men, each with radio-speaker plugs in their ears, stood outside.

Hamilton Jordan opened the door from the inside. There, quietly smiling, was the president standing in front of his desk.

"Mr. President," I said.

Jimmy Carter had been president of the United States for a little more than four hours. I learned later that I was the first official appointment on his schedule.

Hamilton Jordan departed, and the president sat down in the chair behind the desk. As he talked about my heading up the Veterans Administration, I noticed that his desk looked familiar. Suddenly I realized it was the same one President Kennedy had used, the same one I had stood beside 13 years before. President Carter had ordered it reinstalled.

The president concluded his remarks, arose and escorted me to the door. As we parted I mentioned that I had been in the Oval Office once before. The president grinned and said that this was his second time there too.

"I'll do a good job for you, Mr. President," I promised.

The president indicated that he knew I would, and that he not only wanted me to do a good job for him but also a good job for the veterans of the country. After all, he said, he was one of them.

I rolled out of the West Wing's ground floor entrance and headed for my waiting car. Someone held the door open, and I swung myself from my wheelchair into the passenger's seat. As I got in, I happened to look across the White House lawn toward Pennsylvania Avenue. Little more than a block away was the gutter into which I'd been accidentally dumped on my first sojourn out of Walter Reed Hospital.

Six weeks later, on March 2, 1977, I was sworn in as Administrator of Veterans Affairs.

20

EVERY DAY A CRISIS

When President Truman appointed Omar Bradley to head the VA in 1946, he was asked by a Democratic party official, "Why didn't you give that job to a good Democrat?" Truman calmly replied, "I wouldn't do that to a good Democrat."

The challenge of the Veterans Administration's top job took all the energy and ability I had—and more. It gave me an opportunity to try out new ideas as to how the VA could be led to become a better agency. It challenged me with new questions, like what fresh, new programs can be started that will make the VA the finest rehabilitation facility in the world? How can we aid Vietnam veterans in their readjustment? What should we be doing about the aging WW II veteran?

These are challenging ideas perhaps—especially when they have to be implemented through government processes: another reason why each day I learned something new about my job.

For in the Veterans Administration we had a crisis every day. Some were solved by working long hours. Some needed quick

(This chapter is based on an article that appeared in the October 1978 issue of *Guideposts*.)

action. But there are some crises that are not solvable in a pragmatic way; help is needed from a Power outside ourselves.

One such experience took place in June 1977 when I was three months into my job as Administrator. It happened at 5:30 P.M. on a Friday afternoon at the end of a very difficult week.

I had been staring out of my office window which overlooks the White House and Pennsylvania Avenue. Traffic was heavy as Washingtonians were streaming out of the city for the weekend. Almost everybody in our office had gone home, and I was about to head back to my apartment and relax.

Suddenly my secretary, Frances Lupton, rushed in. "The police are on the phone," she exclaimed. "A doctor is being held hostage by a gunman who says he won't talk to anyone but you!"

My weariness vanished. The call was from a southern city more than a thousand miles from Washington, D.C. A police officer reported that a man named Hank Branley* had walked into a doctor's office brandishing a gun. He claimed he was dying of cancer and felt that he had not been treated fairly by the Veterans Administration. He threatened to blow the doctor's brains out unless someone helped him.

Frances handed me a slip of paper with the doctor's phone number. I dialed it. At the first ring it was picked up and a tense voice answered, obviously Branley.

"Hello," I said, "this is Max Cleland, head of the Veterans Administration."

"I don't believe you!" he yelled. "This is a trick!"

"Then call me back at this number in Washington, D.C.," I said, giving him my office number. "I'll be waiting."

* Name has been changed.

He hung up. Meanwhile, rushing through a tracer on Hank Branley, we found that he had been treated at various VA hospitals around the country for a service-connected stomach ulcer. He also had emotional problems.

I certainly had no medical qualifications to deal with such a situation. However, as a former patient myself, I felt I could identify with Branley and his frustration with a large bureaucracy. But would he call back? I stared out the window as the sun disappeared behind the Washington Monument.

The telephone rang. It was Branley. He seemed convinced now that he was indeed talking to the head of the Veterans Administration.

"I need special treatment, but no one believes me," he shouted. Then he rattled off a string of grievances against veterans' hospitals.

"Friend," I said as calmly as I could, "I know how you feel. I've felt that way myself." I continued talking, attempting to assure him that he wouldn't be hurt if he would just put the gun down, leave the doctor's office, and report to one of our hospitals.

But he continued ranting that no one believed him or cared about him.

About 15 minutes passed, and I was getting nowhere.

"Look," I pleaded, "couldn't we bring you. . . ."

Click! He had hung up.

I sagged in my chair. Had something in the man finally snapped? Was he carrying out his threat to kill the doctor?

Picking up the phone, I dialed again.

An angry "Hello!" greeted me.

Again I approached him as a friend. He retorted that nobody believed him and that he was dying. I kept him talking to let him work out his pent-up emotions.

Suddenly he snarled and the line went dead. I looked up at

my secretary helplessly. My ear burned from the pressure of the phone. My back ached from tension, and my shirt was soaked with perspiration. The office darkened as evening approached.

Word now came on another line that the police had the doctor's office surrounded. They had brought the gunman's brother to the scene. But Branley wouldn't budge.

My heart went out to the doctor. What was he feeling? How long could he stand the strain of being under the muzzle of a gun held by a wild-eyed stranger?

Once more I dialed the number. It kept ringing and ringing. My heart sank. Then a voice answered. It was Branley. He was still adamant, but I sensed time was running out.

Anguish filled me. As I sank back in my chair and listened again to his tirade over the phone, I stretched my hand onto my desk and placed it on a Bible.

The black leather Bible had been given to me by the Veterans Administration chief chaplain when I had come to Washington. I always kept it on my desk. It reminded me of the spiritual principle I was trying to live out: to let go and let God. I did this now. Relaxed. Let it go. Prayed for help.

No great words of wisdom instantly filled my mind. Instead, I blurted out impulsively what I was really feeling. "Hank, I'm kinda tired. How about you?"

The phone was silent for an endless moment. Then in a low tone came the words, "I'm tired, too."

Somehow I had reached him. Excitement roared through me. I straightened and leaned forward into the phone.

"Hank," I said, "how about spending the night in the VA hospital there? Get yourself something to eat and a good night's rest, and let's talk about this in the morning."

There was a pause. "You'll really look into my case?" he asked.

We had made contact. We were two human beings, in touch

with each other at last. "I sure will," I promised. "Look," I continued, "your brother is waiting for you. Why not go outside now and meet him? Then we'll get you a bed and give you that examination and X-ray you want tomorrow, first thing."

"Well," he said, "I'll think about it."

"Okay, Hank, do that," I replied.

I put the phone down with a big sigh. Then we notified the police surrounding the doctor's office.

In a few minutes a call came back. After almost three hours of holding the doctor at gunpoint, Hank Branley had released him unharmed, had surrendered, and was on his way back to the VA hospital.

I sank back in my chair. Reason hadn't worked. Logic hadn't worked. Appeals hadn't worked. A simple touch of common humanity had broken down the barriers. The right words had come because I depended on the truth I discovered that dark, rainy night on Interstate 95, outside Richmond: God is always there—especially when we need Him most.

So in a slow way, my life has come together—physically, mentally, and spiritually. I wanted to be master of my fate. I wanted to run my own life without interference. But in trying to be an island unto myself, I was literally broken into pieces. Shattered.

The putting together of the smashed parts took years, and the strengthening process still continues. But through my crises and defeats I have learned that it is possible to become strong at the broken places. I have also learned that ultimate strength comes from letting go and letting God have His way with my life. And when I fall—when I get broken by life—by seeking Him again, I can become even stronger than I was before.

There is a prayer that expresses this thought beautifully. It is allegedly a prayer of an unknown Confederate soldier and was found in a house in South Carolina after the Civil War. It expresses better than anything else how I now feel about my life:

I asked God for strength, that I might achieve,
I was made weak, that I might learn humbly to obey.
I asked for health, that I might do greater things,
I was given infirmity that I might do better things.
I asked for riches, that I might be happy,
I was given poverty, that I might be wise.
I asked for power, that I might have the praise of men,
I was given weakness, that I might feel the need of God.
I asked for all things, that I might enjoy life,
I was given life, that I might enjoy all things.
I got nothing that I asked for—but everything
I had hoped for.
Almost despite myself, my unspoken prayers were
    answered.
I am among all men, most richly blessed.

AFTERWORD

But what about the other lives mentioned and unmentioned in this book, lives which have touched mine in such a way as to facilitate my healing and progress as I continue the strengthening process? What happened to them? As I think of these people I like to reflect upon what Dr. Albert Schweitzer once wrote about the subtle influence of other people on our lives.

> "I always think that we live spiritually by what others have given us in the significant hours of our life. These significant hours do not announce themselves as coming, but arrive unexpected. Nor do they make a show of themselves. They pass almost unperceived. Often, indeed, their significance comes home to us first as we look back. Much that has become our own in gentleness, modesty, kindness, willingness to forgive, in veracity, loyalty, resignation and suffering we owe to people in whom we have seen or experienced these virtues at work, sometimes in great matters, sometimes in small. A thought which had become an act sprang into us like a spark and lighted a new flame within us. If we had before us those who had been a blessing to us and could tell them how it came about, they would be amazed to learn what passed over from their life into ours."

If I could have before me the number of people whose virtues "passed over from their life" to mine, there would not be room enough in a hundred books to tell the story. The people mentioned (and unmentioned) in this book, though, are special. They have had a powerful impact on me and my struggle to become "strong at the broken places." They would, as Dr.

Schweitzer believed, probably be "amazed" at the impression they made on me. Still, the influence is there. They have all helped in one way or another to strengthen me, enable me, and encourage me to go ahead and live my life after the tragedy of Vietnam. These wonderful people and the good Lord have enabled me to live a fuller life. To them I owe everything. This book is as much about their stories as it is about mine. And where are they now?

Edgar Abbott, my boyhood chum who taught me sports, retired from teaching full-time. He now lives in Vinegrove, Kentucky, where he plays golf and enjoys teaching music fundamentals to private students.

"No Way" Dave Alligood, who underwent so much pain in the Snake Pit with his surgeries and skin grafts, is working with other veterans to end their pain. He is on the staff at the VA Hospital in Roseburg, Oregon. In 1991, Dave, like so many other Vietnam veterans, returned to Vietnam seeking healing and recovery. Dave returned to the U.S. with a lot more than just a healing of his memories. He returned with a Vietnamese girl who he adopted. He has returned to Vietnam since and Dave now has two beautiful Vietnamese daughters.

Major Julia Baker, our chief nurse and chief encourager in the Snake Pit, has since left Walter Reed and retired from the Army. She enjoys the sun and her retirement in Orlando, Florida.

Captain Mike Barry, my old company commander, stayed in the Army. He retired as a Lieutenant Colonel and now lives in Arizona. My old battalion commander when I was with the Signal Unit with the First Air Cavalry Division in Vietnam, Colonel Gentry, retired in Augusta, Georgia. He died a few years ago.

Dewitt and Winnette Buice, who have served as my godparents all my life, and who have been there for me at so many critical moments in my life, retired from their jobs as employees at Southern Railway. They live in Chapin, South Carolina, and devote much of their spare time to their neighbors and their church.

President Jimmy Carter has become the world's foremost citizen for peace and honest elections. He has been nominated for the Nobel Peace Prize continually since leaving the presidency in 1981. President Carter and his gracious wife Rosalynn keep a demanding travel schedule. They spend much of their time at the Carter Presidential Center in Atlanta, but also at their second home in the north Georgia mountains. An excellent woodcraftsman, President Carter has become the foremost volunteer for Habitat for Humanity. President and Mrs. Carter also take a special interest in sports for the physically disabled. They are big boosters of a resort in Crested Butte, Colorado, which teaches the disabled how to ski.

Wilma Clark, the bombshell public relations director for the Baltimore Chamber of Commerce in the 1960s, is now retired and living in South Carolina.

Hugh and Juanita Cleland, my parents, are in their eighties. They enjoy traveling, fishing, gardening, and watching their son on C-SPAN on the Senate floor when he makes a speech.

Jim Cloud, the prosthetic technician who made my first artificial limbs, retired from Walter Reed after taking care of so many of us from Vietnam.

Ralph Coley, my fellow Vietnam veteran and triple-amputee

who taught me how to drive a car, was named Disabled American Veterans National Commander by his fellow American disabled veterans in 1985. In 1986, Ralph was named Handicapped Citizen of the Year. He skis at Crested Butte, Colorado, and shows other disabled citizens how the impossible can be done. He is a retired businessman and lives with his wife in New Smyrna Beach, Florida.

Maury Crallé, who taught me a lot about how to face the fear of combat, retired from the Army as a Lieutenant Colonel. After becoming my chief budget officer during my years at the VA, Maury went on to work for the Army as a civilian employee. He is now the ranking civilian in charge of the Army post at Fort Belvoir, Virginia.

United States Senator Alan Cranston, who helped me become head of the VA during his tenure as Chairman of the U.S. Senate Veterans Affairs Committee, retired from the Senate in 1990. He continues to work for world peace. He is an active participant in a foundation put together by Mikhail Gorbachev for the peaceful resolution of world problems in the post–Cold War era.

Ralph DeGaetano, who made my final prostheses for my legs at the VA Prosthetic Center in New York City, retired from the VA after many years of serving and encouraging veterans like me who came to him as a last resort.

Frances Lupton, my personal secretary at the VA, continued to work for me during my tenure as Georgia's Secretary of State. She is now retired from the State of Georgia. She lives in suburban Atlanta.

Hamilton Jordan, President Carter's right-hand man and former

Chief of Staff in the White House, has survived three types of cancer since he left Washington. He and his wife founded a marvelous camp for children with cancer, Camp Sunshine. Hamilton has written a best-selling memoir of his struggle with cancer, *No Such Thing as a Bad Day*. Hamilton and his family live outside of Atlanta.

Sol Kaminsky, the Secretary of the National Amputation Chapter of the Disabled American Veterans in New York City, who lost both legs in World War II and afterward dedicated himself to serving other amputees like me and showing us that the good life was possible, passed away in 1999.

Pete Lassen, a former Special Forces officer in Vietnam and a former executive director of the Paralyzed Veterans of America in Washington, D.C., who introduced me to Senator Alan Cranston's subcommittee in December 1969 to enable me to tell my personal story of my struggle with the Veterans Administration, left Washington and went back to school. He became an architect and specializes in designing buildings and environments that are accessible to the disabled and are barrier-free. He lives in California.

"Nasty Jack" Lawton, the leader of the Snake Pit crew when I was there, stayed in the Army. He retired as a full Colonel in 1991. He currently continues to serve his country and care for veterans as an employee of the VA National Cemetery System at the VA central office in Washington, D.C. He and his family live in the Washington suburbs.

Hamilton McDonald, my hometown friend who served in Vietnam as an advisor to the South Vietnamese Army in the northern portion of Vietnam in I Corps picking bombing targets along the DMZ, retired from the Army as a captain. He turned down a promotion to Major and a troop command after he found out that the White House, and not commanders in the field, was picking bombing targets in Vietnam. He did not want to lead young Americans into combat and risk their lives under such conditions. He now is a personal representative of the head of a worldwide construction company that is contracting to rebuild the infrastructure of Vietnam. He is working with the very Vietnamese who were his bombing targets over thirty years ago.

Jim Mackay, the former Congressman from Georgia who gave me my first break in politics by allowing me to intern in his Congressional office in Washington, D.C., during the summer of 1965, is retired and lives on Lookout Mountain in Rising Fawn, Georgia.

Gus Mann, my first public relations and advertising assistant who helped me win my first race for public office in my contest for the Georgia State Senate in 1970, died in the early '90s.

Johnny Allem, my first political consultant who advised me in my successful race for the Georgia State Senate in 1970, lives in Washington, D.C. He is still active in local politics.

Bill Hamilton, my first pollster who worked closely with Johnny Allem in the 1970 race, died in 2000.

Belle Jones, who gave me my first political coffee, is retired and lives in suburban Atlanta.

Sammy Neuzof, the double-leg World War II amputee who first showed me that I could walk, died in 1989.

Eddie Griggs, the single-leg amputee friend of mine at the VA Hospital in Washington who survived D-Day and the Normandy invasion, died in the late 1980s.

Carl Nunziato, my double-leg amputee buddy from the Snake Pit who wondered how he was going to survive outside the hospital, returned to his hometown of Youngstown, Ohio. There he has become a role model for others to follow. He was named Outstanding Disabled Citizen for the State of Ohio years ago. He became Vice President of a local bank and has become a devoted volunteer of the Easter Seal Society.

"Big Jon" Peters, my main therapist at the VA, married Dee, my first physical therapist at the VA. Jon went on to become a director of the VA rehabilitation program at the VA Central Office in Washington, D.C. He retired from the VA in 1999, and now works for Dee in the private sector at her physical therapy practice. They live in suburban Maryland.

General Tom Rienzi, whom I served proudly as his first aide-de-camp at Fort Monmouth, New Jersey, retired from the Army as a Lieutenant General and the top-ranked signal officer in the Army. However, before his retirement, General Rienzi spent three years of his nights and weekends preparing himself to become a deacon in the Catholic Church. Tom now is the volunteer Catholic Chaplain at Tripler Army Hospital in Hawaii. He lives there on the island of Oahu in his dream home, which he shares with his lovely and gracious wife Clare.

Walt Russell, my fellow disabled Vietnam veteran with whom I had the pleasure of working as we passed a measure in the Georgia General Assembly making public buildings accessible to the handicapped in the early 1970s, ultimately became chairman of our county commission. In the late 1970s after becoming chairman, Walt retired from politics and entered the practice of law. He is retired and lives in Avondale Estates, Georgia, with his family.

Blaze Starr, who had the courage to come to Walter Reed and make us boys from Vietnam feel special and who entertained us in her club in Baltimore, sold the movie rights of her story to Paul Newman. Later, Newman made and starred in the movie *Blaze*. Blaze is now retired and living in her beloved home state of West Virginia.

Dick Sweet, the battalion commander of the 2/12 Infantry Battalion, the battalion I was the signal officer to as it went into Khe Sanh the day I was wounded, was later awarded the Distinguished Service Cross, the nation's second highest award for valor, for his actions during the Tet offensive. Dick had a promising future in the Army. However, after being promoted to Brigadier General, he retired and came to work with me at the Veterans Administration as my chief in terms of personnel. Many years later, Dick confided in me that the ghosts of Vietnam were too much with him. He felt he was not able to continue in the Army. After the Vietnam War, a book was written by a 2/12 staff officer, Charlie Krohn, who had gone through the Tet offensive as a staff officer with Dick. The book, titled *The Lost Battalion*, details the horror of what Dick Sweet and his battalion went through. Dick Sweet fell on ill health some years ago. He died in the late 1970s and was buried with honors at Arlington National Cemetery.

Burt Westbrook, who advised me on the need to improve the GI Bill in the early 1970s when I was in the Georgia State Senate, is a college professor in Atlanta.

I last saw Butch Domingos, the cheerful single-leg amputee in the Snake Pit who first taught me I could dance, in Texas in the mid-1980s. His family has not heard from him since.

Frank Cameron, who patiently drove me to and from Atlanta so I could have dates while I was still in the hospital, is a small business owner living in suburban Atlanta.

Bill Chapman, my high school friend who has been a role model for me all my life, both growing up in our hometown on the same street and as an Army officer and who was the first person from my home to see me in Vietnam blown up and fighting for my life, is the State Director of my U.S. Senate office in Atlanta.

Colonel Metz, former Chief of Orthopedic Surgery at Walter Reed, retired from the Army and went to work for the VA hospital in Memphis, Tennessee, working with the Spinal Cord Injury Unit there. The timing was such that we were both in the VA system together. His former patient—me!—ended up being his boss. We had many laughs about that one! Colonel Metz died in the late 1970s.

Sandy Campbell, an unsung hero of the "Cast Room" at Walter Reed, where I would be hauled weekly on a stretcher to have my bloody dressings changed and who always gave me words of encouragement, has retired from the Army and lives in Washington, D.C.

Steve Miller, who was my first physical therapist at Walter Reed, left the Army for a career in the U.S. Department of Health and Human Services. He currently works there as an officer in the Health Care Finance Administration. He and I got back together thirty years later when I was sworn into the U.S. Senate.

David Lloyd, the Marine who was first to tend my wounds after the grenade explosion, enjoys fishing in the Chesapeake Bay and raising his two children with his talented wife Mimi, who is a physician in the State of Maryland. They make their home in Annapolis.

Steve Johnson, the Navy Corpsman who was the second person to me on the battlefield after David Lloyd, is still caring for the sick and wounded. He works at a hospital in Texas.

Charlie Walton, who as a Marine on the hill with David Lloyd and Steve Johnson also tended to my wounds, became an Air Force B-52 pilot and retired as a major from the Air Force in 1987. In the mid-'80s, he used the VA Vet Center readjustment counseling program I'd created at the VA to meet his own read-justment needs. He credits it with saving his life. What an irony—he helped save my life in 1968 and I helped save his in the 1980s. After receiving counseling, Charlie went back to school and received a Master's Degree in Counseling himself. He currently is a Vet Center counselor to veterans of all wars out of the St. Paul, Minnesota Vet Center. He and his wife live in Frederic, Wisconsin.

The land on which the 106th General Hospital in Yokohama, Japan, was located was given back to the Japanese government in the early 1970s. The Japanese have built a beautiful park on the site. Hopefully, this is a prophecy of things to come. The Asian Pacific theater saw more American casualties in the twen-tieth century than any other theater of war in our country's his-tory. Here's hoping the twenty-first century sees the construction of more parks for peace than hospitals for war.

ACKNOWLEDGMENTS

To Frances Mitchell Lupton whose loyalty and devotion to me for three decades has been a constant source of encouragement and without whose help this book would never have been possible ...

To Jennie Baker, Arlene Duvall, Gwen Langston, Melinda Moore, and Stacey Walde who graciously helped in the typing of the many versions of the manuscript ...

To Dr. John Gardner who taught me how to write ...

To Jim Mackay, Guy McMichael, Marthena Cowart, Al Mann, Stu Eizenstat, Ed Elson, Gus Mann, June Mann, Jim Mayer, Jon Steinberg, Kandy Stroud, Dr. Charles Standridge, Bill Daniel, Bill Johnstone, and Margaret Shannon who reviewed the manuscript ...

To Lola Oberman who helped me get started on this project ...

To Dick Schneider, Len LeSourd, and Gordon S. Carlson of Chosen Books who worked on this book as a labor of love ...

To Patrick and Annabel Curtis, Nancy Ross, Amy Kimball, and Elaine Iler, for their invaluable help and suggestions ...

To Lawrence Jordan, for always steering me in the right direction ...

To Scott Bard, Tysie Whitman, Burtch Hunter, and the folks at Longstreet Press, for their help in bringing this book back into print ...

To John McCain, for a magnificent foreword to this book— my brother, my friend, my colleague, my hero.

Thank you all.

INDEX